The Official Guide to Medical School Admissions (2016 Edition)

- Published by the AAMC, which administers the MCAT® exam and runs AMCAS® (American Medical College Application Service)

- Comprehensive guide on the medical school application process, including how to apply, how admissions decisions are made, and more

- Key information on how to choose the right medical school for you

- Interactive worksheets to help you keep track of your pre-med progress and make the best decisions during the application process

- Must-know information for career changers and gap-year students

Looking for individual medical school data and profiles?

Take advantage of the **Medical School Admission Requirements for U.S. and Canadian Medical Schools** website, the only comprehensive resource of accurate, verified data that comes directly from the MCAT exam, AMCAS, and medical school admissions offices. Learn more at **aamc.org/msaronline**.

aamc.org/msar

AAMC

...al Colleges
...uite 100, Washington, D.C. 20001-2399

ISBN 978-1-57754...

9 781577 541554

The Official Guide to
Medical School Admissions

How to Prepare for and Apply to Medical School

2016 Edition

Association of American Medical Colleges
Washington, D.C.

The Official Guide to Medical School Admissions
2016 Edition

AAMC Staff

MSAR® Content Specialists
Tami Levin
Director, Pre-Med and Applicant Resources

Nicole Lee
Web and MSAR Content Specialist

Geoffrey Young, PhD
Senior Director,
Student Affairs and Programs

Design and Editing
Douglas Ortiz
Director, Creative Services

Christina Scott
Graphic Design Specialist

Cindy Allen
Senior Editor

Consultants
Amy Addams
Director, Competency-Based Admissions

Norma Poll
Senior Director,
Diversity Policy and Programs

Lesley Ward
Senior Specialist, MCAT Outreach and
Communications

Kelly K. Stazyk
Senior Writer/Editor, Careers in Medicine

Dejanira Cruz
Senior Communications Specialist, AMCAS

Irena Tartakovsky
Manager, Science Policy

Sarah Conrad
Director, Advancing Holistic Review Initiative

Lindsay Roskovensky
Senior Research and Data Analyst, Data Operations
and Services

H. Collins Mikesell
Senior Research Analyst, Data Operations and Service

Julie Gilbert
Senior Education Debt Management Specialist

**To order additional copies of this
publication, please contact:**
Association of American Medical Colleges
Publications Department
655 K Street, NW, Suite 100
Washington, DC 20001
Phone: 202-828-0416
email: *publications@aamc.org*
website: *www.aamc.org/publications*

ISBN (print): 978-1-57754-155-4

ISBN (ePub): 978-1-57754-156-1

ISBN (Kindle): 978-1-57754-157-8

Printed in the United States of America. Revised
annually; new edition available in early spring.

Association of American Medical Colleges

The Association of American Medical Colleges serves and leads the academic medicine community to improve the health of all.

Founded in 1876 and based in Washington, D.C., the AAMC is a not-for-profit association dedicated to transforming health care through innovative medical education, cutting-edge patient care, and groundbreaking medical research. Our members include all 145 accredited U.S. and 17 accredited Canadian medical schools; nearly 400 major teaching hospitals and health systems, including 51 Department of Veterans Affairs medical centers; and more than 80 academic societies. Through these institutions and organizations, we serve the leaders of America's medical schools and teaching hospitals and their 148,000 faculty members, 83,000 medical students, and 115,000 resident physicians.

The AAMC's many programs and services strengthen the world's most advanced medical care by supporting the entire spectrum of education, research, and patient care activities conducted by our member institutions. The AAMC and our members are dedicated to the communities we serve and are steadfast in our desire to earn and keep the public's trust for the role we play in improving the nation's health.

The AAMC develops and administers the Medical College Admission Test® (MCAT®), operates the American Medical College Application Service® (AMCAS®), and provides detailed admission information to medical schools and undergraduate premedical advisors.

Important Notice

The information in this book is based on the most recent data provided by member medical schools at the request of the Association of American Medical Colleges (AAMC).

We edited and, in some instances, condensed the material to meet space limitations. In compiling this edition, we made every reasonable effort to ensure the accuracy and timeliness of the information, and, except where noted, the information was updated as of February 2016. All the information, however, especially figures on tuition and expenses, is subject to change and is nonbinding for the medical schools listed and the AAMC. All medical schools listed in this edition, as with other educational institutions, are subject to federal and state laws prohibiting discrimination on the basis of race, color, religion, sex, age, disability, or national origin. Such laws include Title VI of the Civil Rights Act of 1964, Title IX of the Education Amendments of 1972, Section 504 of the Rehabilitation Act of 1973, the Americans with Disabilities Act, and the Age Discrimination Act of 1975, as amended. For the most current and complete information about costs, official policies, procedures, and other matters, please contact individual schools.

In applying to U.S. or Canadian medical schools, applicants need not go through any commercial agencies. The AAMC does not endorse any organization or entity that purports to help applicants gain admission to medical school, other than undergraduate premedical advisors and medical school admission officers.

AAMC Commitment to Diversity and Inclusion

The AAMC's mission is to serve and lead the academic medicine community to improve the health of all. As the U.S. population ages and grows more diverse and disparities in health care persist, understanding the benefits of diversity and inclusion becomes critical to addressing the health of the nation. The AAMC's commitment to diversity and inclusion in medicine and biomedical research spans more than three decades, demonstrated by ongoing leadership and engagement in activities—starting as early as high school—that promote diversity and inclusion through programs, advocacy, and research. Information about AAMC initiatives is available at www.aamc.org/diversity.

Contents

Figures, Tables, and Worksheets

Worksheets at the end of chapters in this guide are available in fillable PDF format at *www.aamc.org/msar-resources.*

How to Use This Guide

The AAMC works through many avenues to support medical education and help aspiring physicians succeed in their path to medical school. We created this guide to serve as a resource for students who are considering a career as a physician. Each chapter explains one aspect of the medical school admission process, and each is carefully reviewed every year by content experts at the AAMC.

Some of you may choose to read this book cover to cover, while others may prefer to skip ahead to chapters that are most relevant to where you are in the application process. Here are some tips to get the most out of the guide.

Skim the table of contents before you begin reading.
Not everyone takes the same path or is in the same place when they use this guide. You may want to read the chapters in the order that most relates to where you are now and what you need to know to move forward.

Use and update the chapter worksheets.
At the end of each chapter, you'll find a worksheet that can help you with your medical school application. Topics include keeping track of your volunteer experiences, finding individuals to write your letters of evaluation, and determining the right time to take the MCAT exam. You may want to complete some of these worksheets after you read the chapter, or you may want to hold onto them until you're at that phase of the application process. You can make copies or complete them using a fillable PDF form at *aamc.org/msar-resources*.

We encourage you to share your work with your prehealth advisor as you fill the worksheets out. You should have an advisor or a mentor to help guide you through this process. Find out more about the benefits of working with an advisor in Chapter 2, "Academic Preparation." If you do not have a prehealth advisor at your school, you can find one at *www.NAAHP.org*.

Look through the data in this book to understand the national picture.
Part of what will make you a well-prepared applicant will be knowing more about the national applicant and acceptance data. While every applicant is different, and while every medical school accepts applicants with a range of scores and experiences, it can be helpful to see how you compare with other applicants across the country. This will help you to decide, along with your prehealth advisor, when you're ready to apply to medical school. The data in this book come directly from the AAMC Data Warehouse, the AAMC Data Book, the American Medical College Application Service (AMCAS), the Medical College Admission Test (MCAT), and surveys conducted with entering and graduating medical students such as the Graduation Questionnaire (GQ) and the Matriculating Student Questionnaire (MSQ). The data are comprehensively updated each year with the most current information available at the time of printing. Because it comes directly from the source, you can trust that it is the most up-to-date and accurate information available. For more and current information, you can check the AAMC Facts Tables available at *www.aamc.org/facts*.

Check out the Medical School Admission Requirements site when you're ready to look at schools individually.
One of the most important decisions you'll make is where to apply to medical school. The AAMC's Medical School Admission Requirements website provides the most comprehensive, up-to-date information and data. When you're ready to start researching medical schools, tap into this powerful online database of information on U.S. and Canadian medical schools and BS/MD programs. As the gold standard for admission requirement information, this is the only comprehensive resource of accurate and current data that comes directly from the MCAT program, the AMCAS program, and medical school admission offices. Your one-year subscription allows you to search, sort, and save information.

The AAMC has resources to help you, from inspiration through practice.
We've got numerous resources to help you whether you're just beginning to consider a career as a physician or you're in the middle of applying to medical school. Take a look at these pre-med and applicant resources and tell other applicants about them if you find them useful.

- Aspiring Docs
    - o   Aspiring Docs Diaries (*aspiringdocsdiaries.org*)
    - o   Inspiring Stories (*www.aamc.org/students/aspiring/inspiring-stories*)
    - o   Fact Sheets (*www.aamc.org/students/aspiring/community/fact_sheets*)
    - o   Ask a Medical Student (*www.youtube.com/user/AAMCvideo*)
- Financial Aid and Financial Literacy Resources
    - o   Fact Sheets (*www.aamc.org/first/factsheets*)
    - o   Medloans® Organizer and Calculator (*www.aamc.org/services/first/medloans*)
    - o   SALT: Money knowledge for college – and beyond (*www.saltmoney.org/AAMC*)
- Medical College Application Test® (MCAT®)
    - o   MCAT® Essentials (*students-residents.aamc.org/mcatessentials*)
    - o   Official Guide to the MCAT® Exam (*www.aamc.org/students/applying/mcat/mcat2015*)
- American Medical College Application Service® (AMCAS®)
    - o   AMCAS Quick Start Guide (*students-residents.aamc.org/amcastips*)
    - o   2017 AMCAS Manual (*www.aamc.org/amcasmanual*)
- Careers in Medicine (*www.aamc.org/cim*)

Keep up and communicate with us on social media.
One of the best ways to find out about what's going on is to follow us on Facebook and Twitter and to check out our videos on YouTube:

 Facebook: *www.facebook.com/aamcpremed*

 Twitter: *twitter.com/aamcpremed*

 YouTube: *www.youtube.com/user/AAMCvideo*

A note about "MD versus DO" Programs. This guidebook explains the process of preparing for and applying to allopathic medical doctor (MD) programs accredited by the Liaison Committee on Medical Education (LCME). You may have heard of osteopath medical programs that grant doctor of osteopathic medicine (DO) degrees. DO and MD programs have many similarities; both types of physicians are fully certified to practice medicine in the United States after passing board examinations. For more information about osteopath medical schools and admission requirements, see the American Association of Colleges of Osteopathic Medicine site (*www.aacom.org*).

Chapter 1

So ... You Want to Be a Doctor

Arianna Yanes, BA
MD Candidate
Northwestern University Feinberg School
of Medicine
Class of 2019

It's an age-old question: What do you want to be when you grow up?

I've been saying 'a doctor' for years, but am just starting to learn what that entails. With each medical school science lecture, public health discussion, or anatomy lab comes an implicit understanding. Instead of cramming to pass a test or discussing for participation credit, we are learning because patients will depend on us. I was drawn to medicine because of physicians' abilities to improve lives. It may seem like a lot of pressure, but it is my main motivation.

Along with my new perspective on medical school comes an evolving idea of what physicians do. I've encountered doctors who work in administration, run labs, or spend months of each year abroad.

This book will take you through the process of applying for medical school and becoming a doctor. Don't worry if you don't know exactly where you want to take your career yet ... I don't either. The way I see it, once we've decided on medicine, the options are endless.

Tomorrow's Doctors, Tomorrow's Cures®

The dream of becoming a doctor is something that many applicants seem to know from an early age. In fact, a recent AAMC survey shows that half of all medical students who responded to the survey had chosen a medical career before they set foot in undergraduate school—and one in five had made the choice before they even started high school (see Figure 1.1).

Whether you have always known that you wanted to be a doctor or are just starting to consider the idea, being a physician is an extremely rewarding profession. A career in medicine offers numerous opportunities to make a real difference in the lives of countless people.

As a doctor, you are likely to see new life come into the world or provide comfort to those about to leave it. Or you may choose to help build the future of medicine by educating the next generation of physicians. Perhaps you will dedicate yourself to discovering new cures for devastating diseases.

Figure 1.1. When did you decide to study medicine? Most applicants knew early on that they wanted to be a doctor.

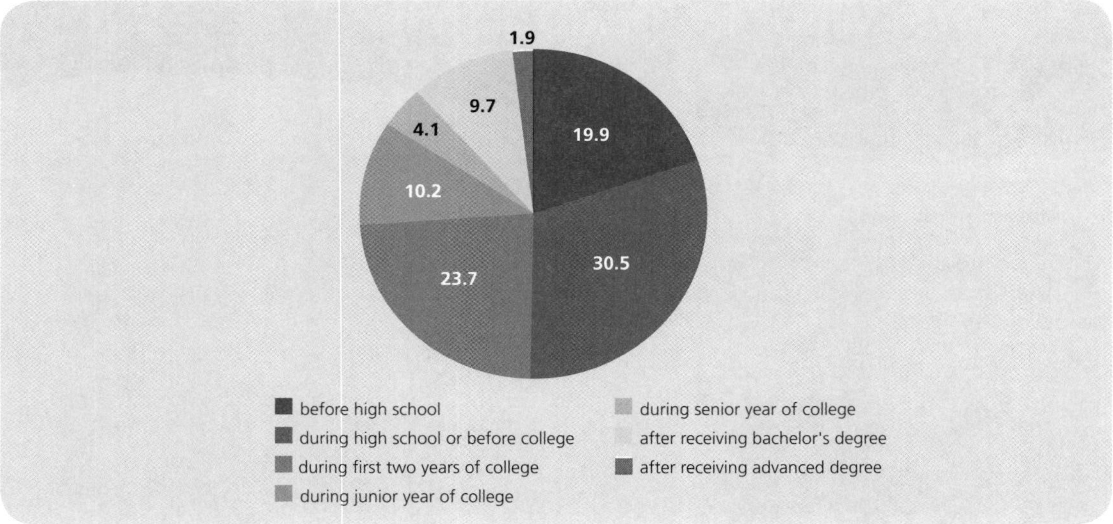

before high school   during senior year of college
during high school or before college   after receiving bachelor's degree
during first two years of college   after receiving advanced degree
during junior year of college

Source: AAMC's 2015 Matriculating Student Questionnaire (MSQ).

Whichever direction you follow, you will—either directly or indirectly—reduce or eliminate people's pain and suffering, improve their quality of life, and provide invaluable service to your local community or the country as a whole.

Your Medical Career Driven by Your Interests

Another benefit of the field is that you can choose from many and varied ways to practice. From clinical practice to biomedical research, from public health to medical education—the choices are plentiful (see Figure 1.2). Medical students typically have clear preferences for the areas they plan to specialize in after graduation. Many students change or further refine their specialty preferences as they gain experience and knowledge in medical school. If your interests change with time and experience, medicine—because of its emphasis on lifelong learning and ties to research and technological developments—will provide you with opportunities to refine your skills and reorient your practice. Here are some examples of possible career options:

- The satisfaction of long-term patient relationships is one attraction of **family medicine and internal medicine**, where the bulk of time is spent in direct contact with patients. Physicians who work under the umbrella of "primary care" often care for entire families and enjoy the challenges that come from treating a diverse population with varied backgrounds and conditions.

- Other physicians may prefer to pursue detailed knowledge about the intricacies of a single organ or system, such as that required of **cardiologists, ophthalmologists, dermatologists, endocrinologists,** and other specialists.

- Interested in **scientific exploration** and the desire to **break new ground in medical knowledge**? Physicians with these interests are found in the nation's private and public laboratories and research institutions.

- Those with a commitment to social justice and an interest in fulfilling the health care needs of the underserved and disadvantaged can meet those challenges **in urban and rural clinics, in public health, or as medical missionaries**.

- Careers in **general surgery** often suit people who have a desire to see immediate results of their interventions. **Plastic and reconstructive surgery** draws others with artistic skills and aesthetic interests.

- Those interested in mind-body interactions and the emotional lives of their patients might find a home in **neurology or psychiatry.**

- The fast pace of medicine draws some to work as **emergency physicians or trauma surgeons**.

- Others motivated by the interest of national defense may use their skills as **flight surgeons or in military medicine**.

- The **economic and public policy aspects of health care** guide some physicians to think tanks and health-related organizations, as well as to serve in the legislative and executive branches of government.

- For those fascinated by the issues facing groups of patients with age-defined illnesses and problems— from the risks in infancy and early childhood to the challenges of older life—fulfillment can come in careers as **pediatricians and geriatricians**.

- Assisting patients in overcoming complex fertility and gestational problems is the hallmark of the specialists in **reproductive endocrinology and obstetrics and gynecology**.

- Those dedicated to reducing the incidence of birth defects and inherited diseases might find their calling in **medical genetics**.

- The detection, prevention, and eradication of injury and disease draw people to the fields of **preventive medicine and epidemiology**.

Figure 1.2. What specialties were entering medical students considering in 2015?

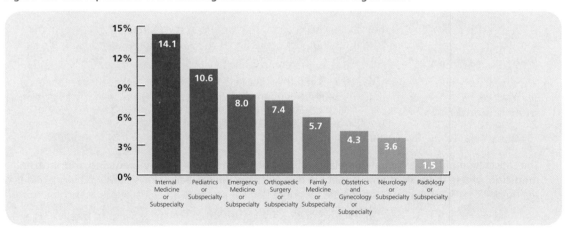

Source: AAMC's 2015 Matriculating Student Questionnaire (MSQ).

Once you enter medical school, you'll start actively learning about these and the myriad other career options and considering where you best fit. This is addressed further in Chapter 3, in the section "Determining How You Want to Practice Medicine."

What About the Future?

As long as we're looking ahead, let's look way ahead. In 5, 10, 15 years, what will medicine look like?

One thing is certain—the face of medicine changes continually. A good example of this has to do with the prevalence of women in medicine. In the 1976–1977 academic year, women made up just 24.7 percent of all medical school matriculants. Compare that with 2014–2015, when they made up almost half—47.8 percent—of the entering class, according to the AAMC Data Book.

Medical students taking the Hippocratic Oath, 2015.

Look back one generation, and you can see that many new fields have emerged.

- An excellent example dates back to the early 1980s. Back then, a new—and fatal—illness was taking hold that nobody could identify. We now know it well: AIDS. **Infectious disease** is currently a large medical subspecialty, and, as a result, significant advances have been made in extending the lives of those infected with HIV.

- Other advances are more recent. **Minimally invasive surgery**, in which surgeons carry out precise procedures sometimes with the assistance of a robot, is becoming increasingly popular. Such surgeries are currently available and used in procedures on lungs, the esophagus, the prostate, the uterus, and kidneys. Through surgeries like these, patients are likely to benefit from smaller incisions, lower risk of complications, shorter hospital stays, less pain, and speedier recoveries.

- A career path unavailable to the previous generation, **personalized medicine**, is a field where the technology allows physicians to identify mutated genes and alert patients about their predisposition to a specific disease. (The next step—actually treating diseases with genes—is on the horizon.)

- Then, there are the more established fields that have evolved to take on new applications. Radiology, for example, is no longer about just reading X-rays. Radiologists can now perform surgery as part of **interventional radiology**.

Even more exciting is what lies ahead: gene therapy, portable medical records, distance surgery, and focused medication. The possibilities for advancement in medical research are limitless.

- Early tests of **gene therapy** have been especially favorable for cystic fibrosis, in which the correct CFTR gene is transported via a harmless virus or liposome.

- Similarly, research is under way in the field of **pharmacogenomics**, in which patients' treatments are tailored according to their specific genetic code. For example, if a patient's genes fit a certain type of cancer code, the physician will prescribe the "matching" pharmaceutical that has been developed to destroy cells with that code—and will know, rather than hope, that the treatment is likely to work. Still in its infancy, most forms of tailored drugs are used in oncology, but studies are progressing in areas of cardiology, diabetes, psychiatric disorders, and more.

- Also in development is **focused preventive care**, which uses genetic diagnosis to identify to a very specific degree how likely a patient is to develop a certain disease or condition—and then prevents that development before it has a chance to begin.

- Other advances will be administrative in nature; the days of hunting down medical records may come to an end, for example. One possibility being explored is a **portable medical records** system, or a national online database of individual health records. Everyone will carry a smart card (or have a microchip inserted under his or her skin!), allowing physicians to access medical records. The benefit? Errors are reduced, files can no longer be lost, delays are minimized, and the experience of having repeated—that is, unnecessary—tests is eliminated.

Workforce Issues

Above all, know this: Whatever specialty you choose, your services as a physician will be needed.

According to a study commissioned by the AAMC, there will be a shortage of 61,700 to 94,700 physicians by 2025. The shortage is being driven in large part by the rapid expansion of the number of Americans age 65 or over. Our doctors are getting older, too. Nearly one-third of today's physicians will be of retirement age in the next decade, just as more Americans need care. A continued demand for physicians and other medical professionals is projected.

Figure 1.3 illustrates the growing physician shortages between 2014 and 2025. Still, the shortages will be experienced unevenly, and some geographic areas will feel the effect more strongly than others. With that in mind, you might consider the trends as you think about the direction you'd like your career to take.

Primary Care

Although the nation is facing an overall shortage of physicians, many people are particularly concerned about the growing deficit of primary care doctors. To encourage more U.S. medical school graduates to pursue a career in primary care, the government is exploring ways to value primary care efforts more fairly and lessen administrative burdens associated with general medicine. You may want to explore the rewards this type of care offers, including the satisfaction that comes from delivering comprehensive care and having long-term relationships with your patients.

Underserved Areas

The impact of this shortage is expected to be greatest in underserved areas—the urban and rural areas where health care is already scarce. If you choose to serve in a community designated as a Health Professional Shortage Area by the U.S. Department of Health and Human Services, you may be able to take advantage of a federal program—the National Health Service Corps—that offers scholarships and loan repayment. According to the AAMC's 2015 Matriculating Student Questionnaire, nearly 26 percent of entering students planned to work in a primarily underserved area, and more than half of all entering students hadn't yet decided where they wanted to work. (Learn more about this program in Chapter 10, "You Can Afford Medical School.")

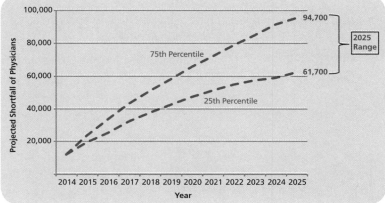

Figure 1.3. Projected physician shortfall range, 2014–2025.

Source: AAMC Center for Workforce Studies, 2016 (www.aamc.org/2016projections).

A More Collaborative Approach

As Congress explores various scenarios as it moves forward with instituting health care reform, one thing is nearly certain: Given the projected shortage of physicians, we will need to develop new models of health care delivery that make better, more efficient use of all health care professionals—not just doctors. That means you can expect to work within a more collaborative, "shared" environment, in which a team of health care providers—physician's assistants and nurse practitioners, for example—work more in tandem. Exactly how that will play out is still in development, but the goal is to create a more efficient system, increase patient satisfaction, and, ultimately, improve health outcomes.

A collaborative approach to health care delivery is instilled beginning in the early years of medical education. Read more about the use of small-group discussions, problem-based learning, and other educational models in Chapter 3, "Your Medical School Years: The Education Process."

Immediate Steps That Lie Ahead

That's the future—or at least what we expect. Right now, though, you're undoubtedly more focused on the short-term goal of getting into medical school.

So what *is* the process for applying to medical school? What lies ahead?

Let's be candid. Getting into medical school isn't easy. (But it's definitely doable—as the more than 76,000 students currently enrolled can testify!) You will need to prepare for and take the MCAT® exam, select schools to apply to, complete the application process, write a personal statement, gather letters of evaluation, secure your undergraduate transcripts, and interview. And then you will wait for notices of acceptance and make your final decision. If you're not accepted, you'll need to evaluate your options and figure out what to do next. All of this will be covered in the following chapters.

But first, right now, you can take many steps to make yourself a more attractive candidate to admission committees. From taking the necessary courses to working effectively with your pre-health advisor to participating in extracurricular and volunteer activities that demonstrate your true interest in medicine, there's a lot you can do.

In the next chapter, we focus on your undergraduate preparation.

A Note for Career Changers or Gap-Year Applicants

If a year or more has passed since you graduated from college, you're not alone. Well over half (59.9 percent) of matriculating medical students indicated in the AAMC's Matriculating Student Questionnaire that there was a gap between their college graduation and matriculation to medical school of at least a year. Medical schools do not see a break between the end of college and beginning of medical school as a weakness or negative attribute. In fact, what you've experienced or accomplished during this time may enhance your application and qualifications significantly.

We'll add tips and things to consider throughout this book to help guide you through the application and preparation process. We know there may be some variation in how you'll need to prepare yourself and compile the different components of your application now that you're no longer on campus.

 Worksheets at the end of chapters in this guide are available in fillable PDF format at www.aamc.org/msar-resources.

Advising Office

Your pre-health advisor*: _____

Advising office phone number: _____

Advisor's email address: _____

Office location: _____

*If your school does not have pre-health advising or you don't have access to an advisor, see the National Association of Advisors for the Health Professions' (NAAHP's) Find an Advisor service (*www.naahp.org/StudentResources/FindanAdvisor.aspx*).

Clubs and Volunteer Opportunities

Pre-med club or society on campus: _____

Pre-med honor society: _____

Service organization club or fraternity: _____

Other Ideas to Make Contacts and Get Experience:

❏ Contact science department about lab and/or research opportunities.

Notes: _____

_____

_____

❏ Contact local clinic or health service provider for volunteer, paid, part-time, or internship opportunities.

Notes: _____

_____

_____

❏ Contact health care providers you know about shadowing opportunities.

Notes: _____

_____

_____

_____

Chapter 2

Academic Preparation

> Our paths to the MD degree begin early. For me, it started when my mom encouraged me to take chemistry during my freshman orientation. I registered for that class, but I had doubts about medical school. I didn't like the sight of blood, and I wasn't great at biology.
>
> My dream seemed distant until Dr. Isaac Yang shared his journey with me. He didn't talk about grades, MCAT scores, or extracurricular activities. Instead, he shared a life-changing experience when he saved a child from a traumatic brain injury on the streets of San Francisco. Years later, that same doctor worked with me to co-edit a book of memoirs, The Service Minded Physician.
>
> It's easy to view the journey to medical school as a contest, but it's really about people. Think about why you're reading this book and the kind of person you want to be beneath your white coat. In this chapter, you will learn about how to build a strong foundation during your education. I'll see you on rounds in a couple years.

Matthew Rosenstein
MD Candidate
Duke University School of Medicine
Class of 2018

Premedical Preparation

College coursework plays a major role in your preparation for medical school. Your major field of study, the mastery of specific scientific principles, and advanced coursework all contribute to that preparation. Let's take a closer look at each of these.

Choice of Major

Contrary to what many college students believe, there is no such thing as the "best" major. **In fact, no medical school requires a specific major of its applicants**. That's because admission committee members know that students develop the essential skills of acquiring and synthesizing information through a wide variety of academic disciplines and, therefore, should be free to select whichever major they find interesting and challenging.

Even so, many premedical students choose to major in a scientific discipline. If that's the direction you're heading in, and you're doing so because you are fascinated by science and believe that such a major will be the foundation for a variety of career options, great. If you're doing so because you believe it will enhance your chances for admission, think again.

Admission committees welcome students whose intellectual curiosity leads them to a wide variety of disciplines.

And no … you won't be at a disadvantage if you choose to major in English, for example, rather than biology. You may be surprised to learn that there is very little difference in median total MCAT® scores among those who major in the humanities, social sciences, and biological sciences. The MCAT and GPAs for Applicants and Matriculants to U.S. Medical Schools by Primary Undergraduate Major, 2015-2016, facts table shows that students from many different majors are accepted to medical school, as long as they have the basic science preparation (*www.aamc.org/download/321496/data/factstablea17.pdf*).

College students take advantage of a variety of programs to prepare for medical school and a career in medicine. Table 2.1 shows the percentage of students who participated in several popular programs.

Table 2.1. How Do Students Prepare for Medical School?

Program	Proportion of Students
Volunteered in the health care field	92.1%
MCAT® preparation course	58.6%
Laboratory research apprenticeship	59.9%
Summer academic enrichment	14.6%
Nondegree postbaccalaureate program to complete premedical requirements	9.7%
Nondegree postbaccalaureate program to strengthen academic skills	6.6%

Source: AAMC's 2015 Matriculating Student Questionnaire (MSQ).

Scientific Preparation

Still, medical schools recognize the importance of a strong foundation in mathematics and the natural sciences—biology, chemistry, and physics—and most schools have established minimum course requirements for admission. These courses usually represent about one-third of the credit hours needed for degree completion (leaving room for applicants to pursue a broad spectrum of college majors, as shown in Figure 2.1. In particular, medical schools expect that their entering students will have mastered basic scientific principles by successfully completing one academic year (two semesters or three quarters) of biology and physics and one academic year of general chemistry and one year of organic chemistry, including adequate laboratory experiences. Increasingly, biochemistry is strongly recommended by schools, too.

Figure 2.1 presents information about the undergraduate majors of all medical school applicants to entering classes for the years 2011–2015. Over the past five years, more than half of all applicants reported undergraduate biological science majors, while the remainder reported a variety of majors, including the humanities, mathematics and statistics, physical sciences, social sciences, and other health sciences, and a broad "other" category. The proportion of these majors has remained relatively constant over time, despite annual fluctuations in the numbers of applicants.

Although only a few medical schools require applicants to complete a specific course in mathematics, all schools appreciate that mathematical competence provides a strong foundation for understanding basic sciences. A working knowledge of statistics helps students fully grasp medical literature, and familiarity with computers is valuable as well. Many medical schools therefore recommend coursework in mathematics and statistics in addition to the science courses named above. Table 2.2 gives an overview of the most common courses required by medical schools.

AP, IB, and CLEP Courses

If you intend to apply college credit earned through **advanced placement (AP), international baccalaureate (IB), and college-level examination placement (CLEP)** to meet premedical requirements, you should be aware that some medical schools have requirements involving the use of such credit. Please review the Medical School Admission Requirements® (MSAR®) website (*www.aamc.org/msar*) and the websites of medical schools you're interested in for more information.

Figure 2.1. Undergraduate major distribution, all applicants, 2011–2015.

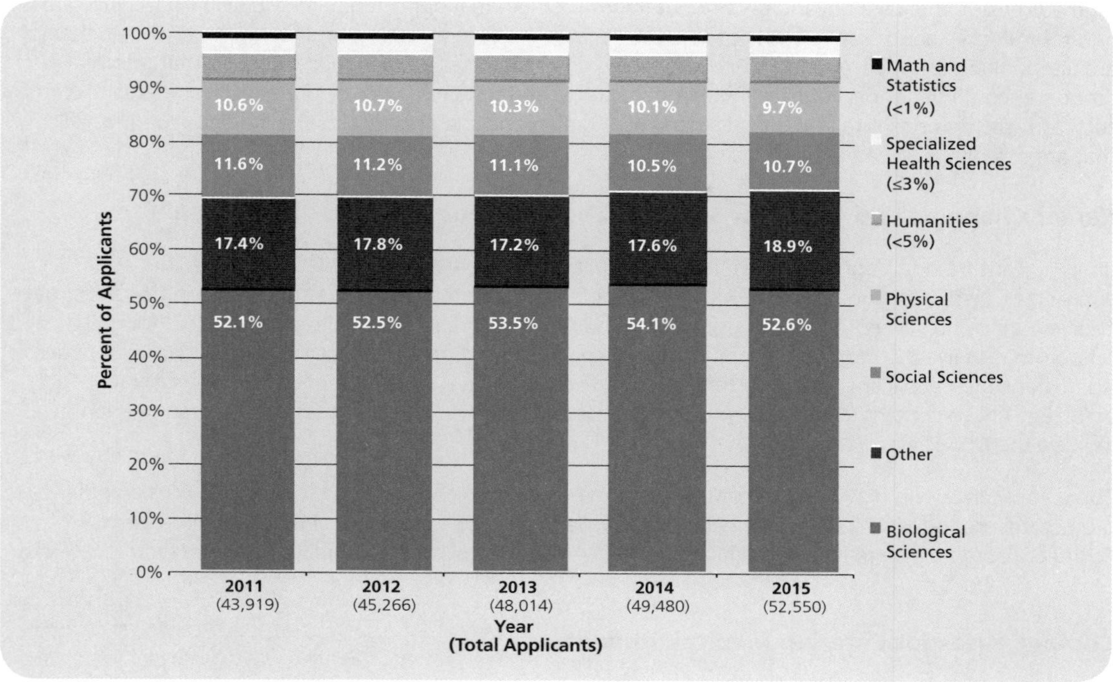

Source: AAMC Data Warehouse: Applicant Matriculant File.

Competencies versus Courses

Finally, for those of you reading this in the early years of college (or in high school), we would like to draw your attention to the fact that medical schools are increasingly defining their prerequisites by competencies—rather than courses. This comes about because, as a study undertaken by the Howard Hughes Medical Institute (HHMI) and the AAMC points out, the scientific knowledge medical schools seek in their applicants can be obtained in a variety of courses as opposed to specific ones. In other words, a student might be able to master chemistry principles in a zoology class or statistics in a sociology class. (The report of that study, *The Scientific Foundations for Future Physicians*, is available at *www.aamc.org/scientificfoundations*.)

Advanced Coursework

Although upper-level science coursework may not be required by every medical school, it's usually a good idea to show that you have challenged yourself academically. Successfully completing advanced courses demonstrates science proficiencies and ultimately strengthens your preparation for medical school. Taking science courses that simply duplicate basic content, however, is not recommended. But don't think that all your courses must

Table 2.2. Subjects Required or Recommended by 10 or More U.S. Medical Schools

Required or Recommended Subject	Number of Schools*
Biochemistry	45
Biology	94
Biology/Zoology	27
Calculus	11
College Mathematics	37
English	78
Humanities	15
Inorganic Chemistry	111
Organic Chemistry	113
Physics	110
Social Sciences	15

*n=145. Some medical schools use a "competency" model that recommends competencies rather than specific coursework. For premedical coursework required by the medical schools you're interested in, please see the Medical School Admission Requirements website (www.aamc.org/msar).
Source: AAMC Medical School Admission Requirements website, 2016.

be STEM-based (science, technology, engineering, and math). Practicing physicians often suggest that premedical students take advantage of what might be their final opportunity for study in nonscience areas and take elective courses in subjects of interest, such as music, art, history, and literature. Medical schools are also looking for applicants with rich and varied coursework and experiences. Beyond that, medical schools encourage honors courses, independent study, and research work by premedical students. Activities such as these demonstrate in-depth scholarly exploration and the presence of the lifelong-learning skills that are essential to a career in medicine.

Career Changers and Gap-Year Students: Not All Coursework Is "Evergreen"

It's important for applicants who have had a significant break between completing coursework and applying to medical school to check with the schools or look in the MSAR site for details on the oldest date coursework can be accepted. This is especially important for core premedical requirements, though some schools may waive the requirement for individual courses based on an applicant's professional experience (for instance, an applicant whose current work shows a high level of competency in a medically related area). Be sure to contact the schools you're interested in or check their websites for their requirements, or look on the MSAR site.

Some applicants who may need to complete numerous courses choose to do so via postbaccalaureate premedical programs for career changers or for those who need to enhance their academic record. Postbaccalaureate information is available on the AAMC's free postbaccalaureate database (*apps.aamc.org/postbac/#/index*).

Competencies for Entering Medical Students

The AAMC's Core Competencies for Entering Medical Students were developed to highlight the knowledge, skills, values, and attitudes that the medical education community thinks are fundamental for students and future physicians. The competencies fall into four categories: Interpersonal, Intrapersonal, Thinking and Reasoning, and Science (*www.aamc.org/initiatives/admissionsinitiative/competencies*). One of the most essential core competencies is **Cultural Competence**, which states that applicants should:

- Demonstrate knowledge of sociocultural factors that affect interactions and behaviors

- Show appreciation and respect for multiple dimensions of diversity

- Recognize and act on the obligation to inform one's own judgment

- Engage diverse and competing perspectives as a resource for learning, citizenship, and work

- Recognize and appropriately address bias in themselves and others

- Interact effectively with people from diverse backgrounds

The AAMC-HHMI Scientific Foundations for Future Physicians report proposes scientific competencies for future medical school graduates and undergraduate students who want to pursue a career in medicine, including these:

- Both the knowledge of and ability to apply basic principles of mathematics and statistics, physics, chemistry, biochemistry, and biology to human health and disease

- The ability to demonstrate observational and analytical skills

- The ability to apply those skills and principles to biological situations

The scientific competencies have been incorporated into the AAMC's Core Competencies.

Personal Attributes

As the Core Competencies for Entering Medical Students suggest, academic and scientific accomplishments alone are not sufficient for a student to be accepted into medical school. While intellectual capacity is obviously important to be a successful physician, so are other attributes that signify the ability to develop and maintain effective relationships with patients, work collaboratively with other team members, act ethically and compassionately, and in many other ways master the "art" of medicine.

The AAMC publication *Learning Objectives for Medical Student Education: Guidelines for Medical Schools* describes the personal attributes required of a physician *(www.aamc.org/initiatives/msop)*. While making note of the fact that graduating medical students must be knowledgeable about medicine and skillful in its application, the publication also emphasizes how vital it is for students to:

- Make ethical decisions

- Act with compassion, respect, honesty, and integrity

- Work collaboratively with team members

- Advocate on behalf of one's patients

- Be sensitive to potential conflicts of interest

- Be able to recognize one's own limits

- Be dedicated to continuously improving one's knowledge and abilities

- Appreciate the complex nonbiological determinants of poor health

- Be aware of community and public health issues

- Be able to identify risk factors for disease

- Be committed to early identification and treatment of diseases

- Accept responsibility for making scientifically based medical decisions

- Be willing to advocate for the care of the underserved

Chances are, some of the most valuable traits you'll demonstrate as a physician are not going to be learned in a classroom. These characteristics may be nurtured throughout your college years (and, as you will see in Chapter 8, are among the attributes that admission officers seek when admitting applicants to their programs). You don't need formal programs to learn how to be a kind, empathetic physician. You'll have an abundance of opportunities to develop these qualities through your interactions with friends, classmates, and others while in college and through your life, work, and volunteer experiences.

Extracurricular Activities Related to Medicine

Your undergraduate years offer opportunities to become involved in a wide range of extracurricular activities. Ideally, at least a few of them should involve the medical field. Experience in a health care setting, such as volunteering at shelters or clinics or in other environments to care for ill or elderly people in your community; participating in basic or clinical research efforts; working as an emergency medical technician; "shadowing" a physician; and providing support to people in a rape crisis center, emergency room, or social service agency are all types of activities recommended to those considering a career in medicine.

These pursuits give you the chance to learn more about the medical profession—and yourself. You will, for example, be able to:

- Explore different interests

- See if you enjoy working in different environments

- Better understand the nature of medical practice and the daily demands placed on physicians

- Assess your ability to communicate and empathize with people from different backgrounds and cultures

- Evaluate your willingness to put others' needs before your own

While this self-analysis can help you decide if a career in medicine is right for you, your involvement with clinical or research activities helps demonstrate to admission committees where your interests lie. It also shows that you have explored various aspects of the medical field.

Admission committees evaluate your experiences using at least three different criteria, and a greater value is assigned to some types of pursuits than others. Specifically, admission committees look at the length of time you've invested, the depth of the experience, and lessons learned—in relation to any particular activity. This means a single, daylong blood drive or one-time-only shadowing experience is perceived as less enlightening than semester or yearlong commitments. By the same token, active participation in an activity is viewed as more instructive than passive participation (such as observation). Most important, admission committees want to know what students learned from their experiences. You should be prepared to address these kinds of questions about your community, clinical, or research experiences in your application materials (which will be discussed in Chapter 7, "Applying to Medical School").

Do *not* approach your extracurricular activities with the idea of "checking off" a wide range of pursuits to impress admission committees. Three or four in-depth experiences from which you gained valuable lessons are far more significant—and telling—to admission officers than dozens of short-term involvements.

Pre-Health Advisors

Fortunately, you're not on your own when it comes to preparing for medical school. Valuable resources are available to you—some of which are likely to be right on campus, including your pre-health advisor.

Depending on the individual school, pre-health advisors work on a full- or part-time basis and may be a faculty member (often in a science department), a staff member in the office of an academic dean or in the career center, the director of an advising office for preprofessional students, or a physician in part-time practice. Advisors belong to organizations such as the National Association of Advisors for the Health Professions (NAAHP, *www.naahp.org*) that assist them in their work—and help them help you. If your school does not have a pre-health advisor, contact the NAAHP about getting a member volunteer to help you. Visit *www.naahp.org/StudentResources/FindanAdvisor.aspx* for more information. You can find a link to each school's admission requirements page here, *students-residents.aamc.org/choosing-medical-career/article/required-premedical-coursework-and-competencies*, and you can use the Medical School Admission Requirements website to view each school's admission requirement profile. You can always reach out to medical school admission staff if you have specific questions about admission requirements or policies. Be sure to check the medical school's website first, though, to see if the information is available there.

Kinds of Services Provided

The support provided by pre-health advisors varies from school to school. Be sure to contact your school's advisor to find out which services and resources are offered.

Generally speaking, services fall into five categories:

- **Academics.** Advisors are well-informed about premedical coursework on their campuses and often work with faculty at their schools to develop suitable academic programs for pre-med students. They collaborate with campus academic staff to design study, reading skills, and test-preparation workshops; offer tutoring programs; and inform students they advise about regional and national programs likely to be of interest.

- **Clinical and research experiences.** Advisors often work with advisory groups composed of college and medical school teaching and research faculty and community clinicians who help applicants identify part-time jobs, volunteer positions, and opportunities for independent study credit in local laboratories and offices.

- **Advising and support.** Advisors help students pursue realistic goals and maximize their potential, both meeting with them individually and providing group opportunities for students to meet with one another. Advisors often establish peer advising and mentoring programs and are particularly sensitive to the needs of students who are underrepresented in medicine or are the first in their family to attend college.

- **Assistance to student organizations.** Advisors coordinate the activities of local and national organizations that serve pre-med students by planning programs, identifying funding sources, and arranging for campus visits from admission and financial aid officers.

- **Sharing resources.** Being aware of students' need for timely and pertinent information, advisors disseminate publications and other resources from relevant organizations, including the AAMC and NAAHP. In addition, advisors provide computer access to Web-based content on health careers programs and educational financing; distribute information about local, regional, national, and international research and service opportunities; and stock a library of publications related to medical school and medical education.

A Wide Range of Guidance

A pre-health advisor may assist you in many ways, including:

- Identifying courses that satisfy premedical requirements

- Determining a sequence for completing those courses

- Finding tutorial assistance, if needed

- Planning academic schedules to accommodate both pre-med coursework and other educational objectives, such as a study program abroad, a dual major, or a senior honors thesis

- Locating volunteer or paid clinical and research experience

- Strengthening your medical school application

- Preparing for interviews and standardized tests

- Arranging for letters of evaluation

- Determining the most appropriate career paths based on your strengths, values, and life goals

Letters of Evaluation and Committee Letters

There is another vital service that pre-health advisors offer their students (and often their alumni): the pre-health committee letter of evaluation.

This is usually a composite letter written on behalf of a medical school applicant by the college or university's pre-health committee. It presents an overview of the student's academic strengths, exposure to health care and medical research environments, contributions to the campus and community, and personal attributes such as maturity and altruism. In addition, the letter may address any extenuating circumstances that may have resulted in deficits in the student's performance during a course or semester, provide perspective on challenges the student may have encountered, and explain school-specific courses and programs in which the student has participated.

Some undergraduate institutions do not provide composite letters of evaluation but instead collect individual letters throughout the student's enrollment. Then, at the appropriate time, they distribute the letters to the medical schools where the student has applied. Keep in mind that letter of evaluation distribution, practices, and polices vary at each undergraduate institution. It's a good idea to work with your pre-health advising office to clarify how they intend to send letters on your behalf.

Special Programs

Finally, we would like to draw your attention to the following two programs that may be of interest (depending on where you fall in the education process):

Combined Baccalaureate/MD Programs

If you're reading this book during the last year or two of high school, you might want to explore a combined BS/MD program, offered at about a quarter of U.S. medical schools. Graduates of these programs, which range in length from six to nine years, receive both a bachelor's degree from the undergraduate institution and an MD from the medical school. For more details and a list of participating schools, please see Chapter 11 as well as the individual baccalaureate/MD program profiles on the Medical School Admission Requirements website (*www.aamc.org/msar*).

Postbaccalaureate Programs

Perhaps you're at a different stage along the educational continuum and have already graduated from college. If your major was something other than science, it's quite possible that you will need to pursue additional coursework before applying to medical school. Postbaccalaureate programs offered at colleges and universities across the country range from formal one- or two-year master's degree programs to certificate programs. They are available to help applicants who may need to strengthen their knowledge in the sciences, complete required premedical coursework, or enhance their academic background or who are career changers. A searchable database of these programs can be found at *services.aamc.org/postbac*. You can also locate medical schools that have postbaccalaureate programs using the search features on the Medical School Admission Requirements website (*www.aamc.org/msar*).

Worksheets at the end of chapters in this guide are available in fillable PDF format at *www.aamc.org/msar-resources*.

Worksheet 2.1
MSAR® Pre-Med Coursework Progress Tracker

Use this worksheet to keep track of your completed premedical courses. The Medical School Admission Requirements (MSAR) website includes charts of each medical school's premedical coursework requirements (*www.aamc.org/msar*). To compare your completed coursework with all medical schools' requirements, use the My Coursework feature available to MSAR subscribers.

Course	Completed	Enrolled	Needed	N/A*	Notes
Behavioral Sciences					
Biochemistry					
Biology					
Biology/Zoology					
Calculus					
College English					
College Mathematics					
Computer Science					
Genetics					
Humanities					
Inorganic Chemistry					
Organic Chemistry					
Physics					
Psychology					
Social Sciences					

*N/A = not applicable because it's not required.

This worksheet will come in handy when you're writing application essays, tracking your experiences, identifying people to ask for letters of evaluation, and filling out the American Medical College Application Service® (AMCAS®) application. You can fill out the online form at *www.aamc.org/msar-resources*.

Date	Experience	What I did	How this prepares or influences me	# of hours	Contact name email, and phone
[Example] January 15– April 1, 2016	Shadowing	Observed Dr. Addams in primary care role	I was able to observe patient-physician interactions and learned about an electronic medical record system.	25	

Chapter 3

Your Medical School Years:
The Education Process

Edwin Acevedo, Jr., MD
General Surgery Resident
Temple University Hospital
Robert Wood Johnson Medical School
Class of 2015

Every medical student will dedicate themselves to studying, but what does it really take to become a doctor? The short answer is four years of medical school, a three-to-eight-year residency program, and passing scores on the USMLE medical licensing exams.

People say the volume of information you learn in medical school is like "drinking from a fire hose." As a med student, you will go from rapidly absorbing a plate full of books in the preclinical years to feeling like a hunter-gatherer learning on the go during clinical rounds. And just when you think you've got it all figured out, you'll learn in residency that every patient is different—there is no golden script. But yet, the information you gather is applicable in a different way for each patient.

The medical education process is vigorous and always evolving, but this very process has made me further appreciate the beauty and art of medicine. Here, we will cover how medical education has changed over time and what material you can expect to learn.

Undergraduate Medical Education: An Overview

At the core, all U.S. medical schools have the same purpose—to educate their students in the art and science of medicine, provide them with clinical experience, and, ultimately, prepare them to enter the next phase of medical training. That is why every school follows the same basic program, requiring students to acquire a basic foundation in the medical sciences, apply this knowledge to diseases and treatments, and master clinical skills through a series of clinical rotations. (Read more about Canadian medical schools in Chapter 14.)

That doesn't mean that all medical schools are alike. It's often said, "When you've seen one medical school, you've seen one medical school." Each institution establishes its own curriculum and course requirements, so, for example, a particular class required by one institution is an elective course in another. Even when medical schools seem to offer identical courses, the content within them may differ, so some of the material covered in immunology in one school, for instance, is presented in pathology in another. The sequence in which courses are taken—and the method by which the content is taught—may differ as well. Beyond that, the processes by which students are graded also vary from school to school, with some institutions following a pass/fail system, others an honors/pass/fail system, and still others a letter grading system. And just as the culture, campus, and personality of the undergraduate schools you considered differed, they also differ among medical schools. The process you'll use to decide which medical school is the best fit for you and your needs will likely be similar to the one you used to choose your college.

Medical schools must meet very exacting standards to earn (and maintain) accreditation, as established by the Liaison Committee on Medical Education (LCME). The LCME, cosponsored by the AAMC and the American Medical Association, accredits medical school programs that grant the MD degree in the United States (*www.lcme.org*). (Accreditation by the LCME is required for schools to receive federal grants and to participate in federal loan programs. In addition, eligibility of U.S. students to take the United States Medical Licensing Examination® [USMLE®]—a discussion of which appears on page 30—requires LCME accreditation of their school. All medical schools listed in this guide are accredited by the LCME.)

Beyond accreditation requirements, the general educational structure and curriculum of most medical schools are similar. There is significant overlap between what has traditionally been referred to as the "preclinical" and "clinical" years—commonly, the first two and last two years of medical school, respectively.

A Word About Preclinical versus Clinical Years

Students typically concentrate their efforts on the scientific underpinnings of medicine during the first two years and apply and refine that knowledge during a series of rotations during the last two years. However, there is often an overlap in content between these two stages of medical education. It's increasingly common for a student to have some clinical exposure in the first year of medical school. Similarly, during the clinical years, students refine their understanding of underlying medical concepts and apply basic science knowledge. It's important, therefore, to recognize that preclinical and clinical content can—and does—intersect at any stage in the medical school experience.

Building a Foundation of Knowledge

In almost all cases, you'll begin your medical school studies by learning how the human body is supposed to work— in terms of both structure and function. The focus will then shift to abnormal conditions and diseases, methods of diagnosis, and treatment options.

Normal Structure and Function
Before you learn about illnesses and ailments, you'll learn how the healthy body works. That's what you'll be studying right out of the starting gate, and your courses will be many—and varied. Typically, your basic classes will include gross and microscopic anatomy, physiology, biochemistry, behavioral sciences, and neurology.

Abnormalities, Diagnostics, and Treatment
After you've learned what "healthy" looks like (and acts like), the focus of your coursework will shift again, in structure and function. You'll study the full range of diseases and atypical conditions, methods by which diagnoses are made, and therapeutic principles and treatments. It's at this stage that you'll have classes in immunology, pathology, and pharmacology.

Other Topics
You'll be exposed to a wide variety of other topics, such as nutrition, medical ethics, genetics, laboratory medicine, substance abuse, geriatrics, health care delivery systems, research, preventive medicine, human sexuality, and community health, to name a few. The subjects taught at medical schools are as varied, and potentially as numerous, as the institutions themselves.

And that's just part of the picture. There's much more to "building a foundation" than mastering the scientific basis of medicine. During this period of your medical education, you'll learn the basics of taking a patient history, conducting physical exams, interpreting laboratory findings, and considering diagnostic treatment and alternatives—in effect, readying yourself for the clinical rotations that follow in the second half of medical school.

Finally, keep in mind that practicing medicine is not all science—or even the application of science (such as that required to interpret lab results and figure out a course of treatment). Medical schools recognize that physicians practice in a social environment—one in which effective team building, collaboration, and communication skills are necessary. As a result, the very way students learn and are taught has evolved in recent years. (This is discussed in more depth on page 24 under "The Changing Face of Medical Education.")

What a Typical Curriculum May Include

Although the specifics of curricula may differ from school to school, most of them follow the same basic structure. (The list below doesn't include all possible courses and clerkships.)

Year 1: Normal structure and function—Biochemistry, cell biology, medical genetics, gross anatomy, structure and function of human organs, behavioral science, and neuroscience

Year 2: Abnormal structure and function—Abnormalities of structure and function, disease, microbiology, immunology, pathology, and pharmacology

Years 3 and 4: Clinical clerkships—Generalist core: family and community medicine, general and ambulatory care, internal medicine, obstetrics and gynecology, pediatrics, surgery, and research

Other requirements: neurology, psychiatry, subspecialty segments (anesthesia, dermatology, urology, radiology, etc.), emergency room and intensive care experiences, and electives

Acquiring Hands-On Experience Through Rotations

A major component of your undergraduate medical education, typically during the third and fourth years, will be a series of clinical rotations that usually last from four to six weeks each. Under direct supervision of a faculty member, you'll get firsthand experience working with patients and their families in inpatient and outpatient settings.

While the pattern, length, and number of rotations differ from school to school, core clinical training usually includes rotations in family medicine, internal medicine, obstetrics and gynecology, pediatrics, psychiatry, and surgery. Beyond that, and depending on your specific school's requirements, your program may also include clerkships (often referred to as "rotations") in primary care and neurology, for example, or require participation in a community or rural program.

What You'll Do
During a rotation, you'll be assigned to an outpatient clinic or inpatient hospital unit where you'll assume responsibility for "working up" a number of patients each week—collecting relevant data and information from them and presenting findings to a faculty member. Beyond that, you'll participate in the ongoing care of patients, either during hospitalizations or through the course of outpatient treatment. When appropriate, you'll interact not only with the patients themselves, but also with their families.

And What You'll Learn
There's no substitute for hands-on experience—and plenty of it. During the course of your rotations, you'll learn to apply basic science knowledge and clinical skills in diagnosing and treating patients' illnesses and injuries and will become adept at interacting with patients (and their families) as you provide information, answer questions, and prepare your patients for the likely outcome. At the same time, you'll become effective at working with all members of the health care team, whether at the bedside, during inpatient team discussions ("rounds"), or in case-based lectures and small-group discussions.

Electives

Just like college, you'll get an opportunity to explore special interests by way of electives. Offered in basic, behavioral, and clinical sciences, as well as in basic and clinical research, electives are usually available during your final year of medical school (although you might be able to take them at other times). They may be completed on your own campus, at other medical schools through a "visiting student program," through federal and state agencies, in international settings, and through service organizations. The range of activities medical students participate in is broad. The most popular ones are shown in Figure 3.1.

Figure 3.1. The most popular elective and volunteer activities in medical schools, by percent of students who participated.

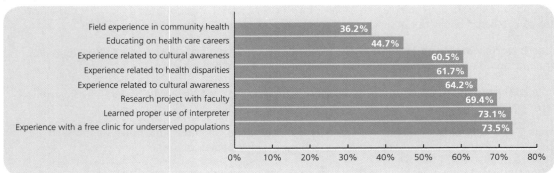

Source: AAMC's 2015 Graduation Questionnaire (GQ).

The **Visiting Student Application Service (VSAS)** is an AAMC online application that helps you apply for senior "away" electives by offering a streamlined, paperless process. You can apply to a variety of elective rotations at participating U.S. institutions by submitting just one application! Clinical away electives provide exposure to new educational experiences and a chance to explore residency opportunities. Speak with the office that helps with your fourth-year schedule about gaining access and starting the application process. Visit the VSAS website for additional information at *www.aamc.org/vsas.*

The Changing Face of Medical Education

You may have heard of Abraham Flexner, who wrote a groundbreaking report on medical education in 1910, when many medical schools were small trade schools unaffiliated with a university and a degree was awarded after only two years of study. Although the basics of his model have survived to the present day—mainly, a four-year program affiliated with a university—he never intended it to serve for more than a generation. After all, no one can predict the future.

Time has certainly proven that this is a successful model.

There's no way that Flexner could have anticipated the shifting demographics, technological advances, and evolving teaching techniques of the late 20th and early 21st centuries. According to the U.S. Bureau of the Census, the U.S. population over age 65 is expected to be almost 74 million by 2030—accounting for 1 in every 5 Americans. Demographics such as that, together with advanced technologies, scientific discoveries, and evolving teaching techniques, all contribute to significant changes in medical education. You'll experience firsthand the reforms taking place in medical education, in terms of both what you'll learn and how you'll learn it. Your courses may range from cultural competency to health care financing, and you'll benefit from educational developments such as computer-aided instruction, virtual patients, and human patient simulation. It's an exciting time to be a medical student.

What You'll Learn

You're going to wield a scalpel in anatomy class early on in medical school, just as students in our parents' and grandparents' generations did 30 and 60 years ago. Certain things stay the same. That type of effort aside, though, there are many significant changes in medical education content, and schools are continually revising their curricula to reflect advances in science, breakthroughs in medicine, and changes in society. For example:

- Consider the demographic shift we'll experience as the baby boomers age. By 2030, the population of people age 65 and over is expected to double, and physicians will spend an increasing amount of time treating age-related problems such as Alzheimer's disease, heart failure, pulmonary disease, and bone disorders. As a result, most medical schools now include in their curricula courses on geriatrics, palliative care, pain management, complementary medicine, and other similar age-based material.

- Issues such as health literacy, nutrition, drug abuse, and domestic violence are now important components of medical education. Because many of these and other health problems are related to culture and lifestyle, medical schools have increasingly focused efforts on areas such as disease prevention, health promotion, population health, and cultural diversity.

- Medical schools are focusing increasingly on helping their students develop more effective communication skills, allowing them to interact successfully with a diverse group of patients. You'll be taught specifically how to assess family, lifestyle, and socioeconomic factors that may influence your patients' behavior or affect their care.

Then, of course, there are the advances in science and medicine themselves. As researchers make breakthroughs in genetic diagnoses and treatments, for instance, that new knowledge is incorporated into the medical school program. There are also expanded courses on medical ethics, examining some of the dilemmas physicians may face amid the advent of new technology; classes on financial decision making, in which students are taught to weigh the likely costs and benefits of various treatments; and sessions on evidence-based medicine and patient quality, providing students with the information and tools they will need to deliver the best possible care. Some examples of topics that are now included in medical education are shown in Table 3.1.

The topics described here are only an overview of some possibilities. The specific courses you'll take as a medical student will vary depending on the school.

Table 3.1. Examples of "New" Topics in Medical Education

Course	Number of Medical Schools Offering the Topic
Medical genetics	140
Cultural competence	139
Communication skills	138
Domestic violence/abuse	138
Pain management	137
Substance abuse	137
Preventive health	136
Health care systems	134
Complementary/alternative health care	126
Health care financing	123

Source: 2014–2015 LCME Part II Annual Medical School Questionnaire.

How You'll Learn It

Do you have an image of sitting in a large lecture hall, surrounded by hundreds of your peers? While you'll certainly experience that aspect of medical school, that method of teaching is being replaced (to a significant degree) by other techniques. Here are a few of the most widespread methods:

- The traditional lecture-based approach is increasingly giving way to student-centered, small-group instruction—similar to the case study teaching method common in both law and business schools. You may be assigned to small groups of students—overseen by a faculty member—in which you'll focus on specific clinical problems. The aim here is to instill medical knowledge and skills, as well as help you build the communication and collaboration skills you'll need as you continue your medical training and, ultimately, as a fully licensed physician.

- Fast-moving technological advances have certainly affected the medical school education program. You'll probably use a computerized patient simulator to apply the basic sciences you've mastered to a clinical context and refine your diagnostic skills. These simulators, which are easily customized to replicate a wide range of situations, are currently part of the curriculum in most medical schools. They are often customized to cover many aspects of a clinical encounter, and they offer medical students easy access to a range of medical situations. Human patient simulators allow students to engage in emotional and sensory learning. These interactive experiences foster critical thought and effective communication.

- Another way medical schools use new technology is with computer-aided instruction and "virtual" patients. Here, you'll apply newfound knowledge and skills via interactive Web-based or software programs that simulate complex cases. Some advantages of computer-aided instruction are that it:

    o   Enables visualizing complex processes

    o   Allows independent exploration

    o   Offers easy access

    o   Costs relatively little

To learn more about the specific teaching methods of the medical schools you're interested in, please see the applicable school listing on the Medical School Admission Requirements website (*www.aamc.org/msar*).

Determining How You Want to Practice Medicine

Required courses. Clerkships. Electives. There's a lot occupying your time and energy as you advance through medical school. At the end of your third year and the beginning of your final year, you'll prepare to apply to residency programs. But before you can apply, you must make some serious decisions about how you want to practice medicine and identify the additional medical training that will prepare you for that work. All this career planning is commonly summarized as "choosing a specialty" and "applying for residency."

Choosing a Specialty

Choosing a medical specialty is one of the most significant decisions you'll make during medical school, and the process can be daunting. No one can prescribe which specialties are best for you. Making a good specialty decision requires you to be proactive. You'll likely begin the process of figuring out which specialties align with your interests, talents, and passions soon after you enter medical school.

The first step in choosing a specialty involves exploring what you want in your medical career. You can do this by:

- Observing and evaluating what you enjoy and what makes you happy across your experiences before and during medical school.

- Objectively considering your career preferences using the Careers in Medicine® (CiM®) self-assessments.

- Engaging in specific activities that can help with the decision, such as shadowing physicians to learn about the work they do and find out whether you'll enjoy it.

As a result of such efforts, you'll better understand your interests, values, skills, and other attributes, as well as your personal, educational, and career goals. This information will be most useful as you gain firsthand exposure to specialties during your clinical rotations, which occur in the third and final year of medical school. These rotations will be your most concentrated opportunity to "try on" different specialties. If by the start of your rotations you've already thoroughly considered who you are and what you want for your career, your rotations will provide much more insight for you.

Applying for Residency

Once you've chosen your specialty or specialties of interest, you must research and select residency programs in those specialties, then compete for a position in those programs. Much like the application process for medical school, you'll complete an application, craft a personal statement, and submit transcripts and letters of evaluation. An application service, such as the AAMC's **Electronic Residency Application Service**® (ERAS®, *www.aamc.org/eras*), usually facilitates this process by electronically sending your application portfolio to your chosen residency programs. The application service(s) you use are determined by the specialty or specialties you're applying to (though ERAS is the application service that includes the most specialties and is used by the most applicants).

Once you've submitted your application portfolio to your chosen residency programs, these programs will review your materials and decide whether to invite you for an on-site interview. Once all Interviews are complete, both residency applicants and individual programs rank their preferences and submit them to a matching service. The matching service runs an algorithm to compare the applicants' list of preferred programs with the programs' list of preferred applicants. After the algorithm runs, you'll learn if you've "matched" to a residency program.

The matching service that includes the most specialties and is used by the most applicants is the **National Resident Matching Program**® (NRMP®, *www.nrmp.org*), which runs its match the third week in March. That Friday—commonly known as "Match Day"—is met with great anticipation, as 17,000 medical school seniors learn where they'll spend the next several years of training. (These 17,000 students are the graduates of medical schools that grant the MD degree. In addition, 18,000 graduates of osteopathic schools [those granting the DO degree] and Canadian and international medical schools compete for residency program assignments through the NRMP. To learn more about ERAS and NRMP, go to *www.aamc .org/eras* and *www.nrmp.org*. There is also a specific match solely for osteopathic medical students through the AOA Intern/Resident Registration program. For more information, go to *www.natmatch.com/aoairp*.)

You can view live-streaming sessions of Match Day ceremonies at many medical schools. Look for links posted on Facebook (*www.facebook.com/aamcpremed*) and Twitter (*@AAMCPreMed*) for more details. Other match programs commonly used by students include (but aren't limited to) the San Francisco Residency and Fellowship Matching Services (*www.sfmatch.org*) and Military Graduate Medical Education (*www.militarygme.org*).

Getting Help

Determining which career path is right for you, as well as navigating the specialty choice and residency application and match process, is a lot for someone to manage alone—and you shouldn't. Many resources and people (including your student affairs office, mentors, and advisors) are available to help you make wise decisions about your future career.

One key resource is **Careers in Medicine** (CiM), a career planning program created by the AAMC and available to medical students and medical schools. Through its website (*www.aamc.org/cim*), CiM provides information, best practices, data, and tools to help you:

- Identify career goals
- Explore specialty and practice options
- Choose a specialty

- Select and apply to residency programs

- Learn to make good career decisions

Here are some examples of what the CiM website offers:

- Self-assessments that help you explore your interests, values, and skills so that you can identify specialties that might fit you well

- A database of clinical and research opportunities available to you during medical school

- Profiles of more than 120 specialties, including

    o   Descriptions of the work

    o   Salary and lifestyle information

    o   Workforce data

    o   Prerequisites and length of training for residency and fellowship programs

    o   Residency interview timing

    o   More than 1,000 links to additional specialty information

- Profiles of more than 9,000 residency and fellowship programs and a tool to help you evaluate programs

- Information about various practice settings

- Lots of guidance and advice

For more information about how to access CiM, visit *www.aamc.org/cim*.

CiM works in conjunction with medical schools' career advising programs. Medical schools are required to provide advisors formally or informally to help students plan their academic and professional career. These services are often organized and delivered by the student affairs office or career center and can include workshops, specialty interest groups and panels, networking receptions, and other career-related resources and opportunities.

Sometime in your first year, your medical school will likely introduce the concept of medical student career planning and explain the advising services it offers. (If you'd like to start exploring your career sooner, contact your school's student affairs office.) Once your third year begins, your school will likely provide more intensive support—for example, by conveying information, including deadlines, about the residency application and match process.

Paying close attention to communications (written and verbal) from your school—especially your student affairs office and advisors—being open-minded and listening to the advice given to you by these individuals, and being proactive in your own career planning will position you to make good decisions and be as successful as possible.

More Medical Training: Graduate Medical Education

Once you've graduated from medical school, you can claim the "doctor" title, but you can't yet practice medicine independently. You're required to progress from undergraduate medical education (that is, medical school) to graduate medical education (GME).

We won't go into detail about postgraduate work here, since you won't need the details until later. But, in a nutshell, the primary purpose of graduate medical education is to give medical school graduates the skills and knowledge they need to become competent, independent physicians in their desired specialty.

Table 3.2. U.S. Residents by Specialty, 2013–2014

Course	Number of U.S. Residents
Allergy and Immunology	304
Anesthesiology	5,668
Colon and Rectal Surgery	83
Dermatology	1,184
Emergency Medicine	5,631
Family Medicine	10,077
Hospice and Palliative Medicine	178
Internal Medicine*	22,971
Medical Genetics	81
Neurological Surgery	1,272
Neurology	2,207
Nuclear Medicine	102
Obstetrics and Gynecology	4,942
Ophthalmology	1,323
Orthopedic Surgery	3,529
Otolaryngology	1,454
Pain Medicine	294
Pathology—Anatomic and Clinical	2,276
Pediatrics	8,592
Physical Medicine and Rehabilitation	1,162
Plastic Surgery	377
Plastic Surgery—Integrated**	495
Preventive Medicine	242
Psychiatry	4,917
Radiation Oncology	686
Radiology—Diagnostic	4,471
Sleep Medicine	126
Surgery—General	7,890
Thoracic Surgery	207
Thoracic Surgery—Integrated**	90
Urology	1,189

*The most popular subspecialties in 2013–2014 in internal medicine were cardiovascular disease (2,598), gastroenterology (1,418), hematology and oncology (1,566), pulmonary disease and critical care medicine (1,494), and nephrology (926).
**Integrated programs differ from subspecialty programs in that they include core surgical education.
Source: AAMC Data Book, 2015, for the 2013–2014 academic year, and AAMC's Careers in Medicine program.

Residency and Fellowship Training

Residency training—the first level of GME—ranges in length from three to eight years (sometimes more) and is necessary for board certification (see Figure 3.2). Residency programs are conducted primarily in clinical settings (for example, in hospitals, outpatient clinics, community health centers, and physicians' offices) and require residents to participate fully in patient diagnoses and treatment. As a resident, you'll work under the supervision of physician faculty as you develop experience in your chosen specialty, become proficient with common and uncommon illnesses and conditions, attend conferences, teach less-experienced colleagues, and generally adjust to the demands of practicing medicine.

Just as medical schools vary, so do residency programs. Depending on the specialty you choose to pursue, you might complete a preliminary year of broad clinical training before focusing on your specialty. This practice is common in anesthesiology, dermatology, and radiology. In other fields, such as family medicine and pediatrics, you'll enter the specialty track directly. (Your medical school advisor and the Careers in Medicine program can provide more information as you approach this stage of your medical education.)

After residency training, you can continue your graduate medical education by completing fellowship training. This second level of GME usually prepares physicians to subspecialize, but some fellowships are for training in other areas, such as research or education administration.

Graduate medical education can be a challenging and rewarding stage of your career. Many physicians look back on their residency and fellowship years as a time when they gained invaluable lessons that they carry with them throughout their career.

Interprofessional Education

The delivery of medical care is increasingly a team-based, collaborative effort that includes doctors, nurses, pharmacists, physical therapists, and other health care providers. Caring for a patient effectively and efficiently depends on practitioners from all disciplines becoming familiar with one another's roles, perspectives, languages, and communication styles.

Because medical educators across the levels of medical education want to help you develop that knowledge and ability, your medical education is likely to involve some form of "interprofessional education." You'll learn to share resources, work as a unit, or participate in other activities that encourage interaction among various categories of health care providers. Through these exercises, you'll all become more adept and successful working as a team and, ultimately, be able to deliver higher-quality patient care.

Licensure and Certification: Ready to Practice Independently

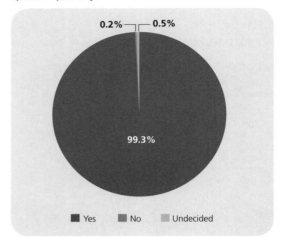

Figure 3.2. Medical school graduates' answers when asked whether they planned to become certified in a specific specialty.

Source: AAMC's 2015 Graduation Questionnaire (GQ).

All medical school graduates must demonstrate command of the same fundamental concepts before becoming licensed physicians. Physicians' mastery of these fundamentals is ensured through the standards of the **National Board of Medical Examiners®** (NBME®) and the **Federation of State Medical Boards** (FSMB). These two bodies jointly sponsor the **United States Medical Licensing Examination®** (USMLE®). This exam is the final assessment of your ability to assume independent responsibility for delivering medical care and is administered in three steps, each at a particular stage of medical education:

- **Step 1:** Usually taken at the end of your second year of medical school, Step 1 tests whether you understand and can apply sciences basic to the practice of medicine. Its focus is on principles and systems of health, disease, and methods of therapy.

- **Step 2:** Many medical schools require you to take and pass Step 2 before you graduate. It's actually two tests in one—the first evaluates your clinical knowledge (CK) and the second your clinical skills (CS). Basically, Step 2 assesses your ability to provide patient care under supervision.

- **Step 3:** After you've completed your first year of residency training, you're eligible for Step 3—the concluding test that determines your readiness to apply your medical knowledge and clinical skills without supervision, with an emphasis on patient management in ambulatory settings.

You can view the USMLE Step Exam polices for the schools you're interested in applying to at the Medical School Admission Requirements website.

After you complete your educational and training programs and achieve passing scores on the USMLE, you can apply for licensure in any of the 50 states, 10 Canadian provinces, 3 U.S. territories, and the District of Columbia.

But … there is one additional step: certification. Although it's not required for medical practice, as licensure from a state or provincial medical board is, certification in a specialty is strongly encouraged (see Table 3.2). Physicians apply voluntarily for this additional credential, which is granted by the American Board of Medical Specialties (ABMS) and involves a comprehensive exam. (Those who have satisfied all ABMS requirements are certified and known as "diplomates" of the specialty board.) Most medical school graduates plan to become certified in a medical specialty (see Figure 3.2).

Continuing Medical Education: Lifelong Learning

Finally, as you likely have realized, your medical education will be a lifelong process. As medicine continues to advance and change, you'll be given the opportunity to learn new skills to stay current with exciting and innovative developments.

The fast pace of change in medicine makes continuing education essential, so most states require participation in accredited continuing medical education (CME) activities. Physicians participate in CME programs throughout their careers, ensuring that they stay up-to-date with the rapid advancements in their specialties and they maintain their clinical competence. Offered by medical schools, teaching hospitals, and professional organizations, these CME programs are reviewed by the **Accreditation Council for Continuing Medical Education** (ACCME) to ensure that high standards are achieved and upheld.

CME reflects a commitment to lifelong learning that's a hallmark of the medical profession. If you're interested in what your CME efforts will entail, go to *www.accme.org*.

 Worksheets at the end of chapters in this guide are available in fillable PDF format at *www.aamc.org/msar-resources*.

First things first: You do not need to know your medical specialty now—or even need to be thinking about it. However, many applicants envision themselves in a particular specialty before day one of medical school. These visions can often be tied to the shadowing or medically related volunteer experiences that many applicants participate in to help prepare for medical school. If you're one of these applicants, it likely means you're already familiar with one or more medical specialties.

Now, the second thing to keep in mind: Changing your mind about what type of physician you want to be is not a sign that you're less committed to the profession. We know from responses to the AAMC's Matriculating Student Questionnaire and Graduation Questionnaire that about 70 percent of medical students change their mind about their specialty choice before they graduate. It's natural and expected that your choices will evolve as you progress through medical school and gain new educational and clinical experiences. So, keep your options open to allow for something amazing you have yet to encounter to inspire you and change your life. And enjoy the reprieve of waiting a little while to finalize your specialty choice.

That being said, if you're an applicant with some exposure to specialties before medical school, you may find it helpful to keep a journal or notes about your experiences while they're fresh in your mind, which you can use once you enter medical school and begin the Careers in Medicine program (*www.aamc.org/cim*). You'll likely find it helpful to refer back to these notes once you've matriculated and as you progress through medical school.

Here are some prompts to help you consider your specialty experiences:

- Do you have a specialty or specialties in mind? _____

   _____

- What is your experience with that specialty? _____

   _____

- Have you shadowed in that specialty with different physicians or in different settings? _____

   _____

- Have you shadowed in more than one specialty? If so, list here: _____

   _____

- Take a moment to compare your experiences. Write down how they were similar and different and how you felt about each. _____

   _____

You can also visit your school's career center for more guidance about exploring medical careers. A career center may be able to help you find shadowing and other opportunities that can expose you to career options. You could also speak with people who have already completed any experiences you're considering.

A note about shadowing: In recent years, due to the Health Insurance Portability and Accountability Act, or HIPAA, it may be more difficult to obtain permission to shadow a physician. There are programs that facilitate paid experiences domestically and abroad. They can be quite expensive. Be certain to check with your pre-health advising office to see if they have experience with a particular program to make sure it's legitimate and safe.

For more information about shadowing, lab, and volunteer experiences, see:

- **Shadowing a Doctor**—*students-residents.aamc.org/applying-medical-school/article/howgetlabexperience*

- **Getting Lab Experience**—*www.aamc.org/students/aspiring/experience/280610/labexperience.html*

- **Finding Health Care–Related Volunteer Opportunities**—*students-residents.aamc.org/applying-medical-school/article/finding-health-care-related-volunteer-opportunities*

Chapter 4

Building Toward Greater Diversity

Tehreem Rehman
MD Candidate
Yale School of Medicine
Class of 2017

> *When I met my medical school peers, I found our varied backgrounds to be fascinating points of discussion; we exchanged thoughts on current health care issues such as mistrust of providers, language barriers, and structural causes of health inequity.*
>
> *Diversity has been shown to enhance the educational experience. It generates a wealth of ideas, helps students challenge their assumptions, broadens their perspectives, and leads to better learning outcomes.*
>
> *Promoting diversity also necessitates recognizing unequal playing fields and extending opportunities to disenfranchised individuals. As a low-income first-generation college student, I would not have been able to attend my current school if it weren't for a merit-based scholarship for disadvantaged students.*
>
> *The AAMC strives to increase diversity among applicants, and many medical schools offer programs to ensure that all candidates have an equal opportunity for admittance. A just representation of historically marginalized communities in both the student body and faculty is ultimately conducive to producing physicians who are socially responsible.*

Defining Diversity

What exactly is meant by "diversity"?

When they hear the word diversity, many people automatically think in terms of race and ethnicity. And while it is certainly important to have more racial and ethnic minority populations represented in medicine, the concept of diversity is much more expansive.

Diversity refers to the richness of human differences—socioeconomic status, race, ethnicity, language, nationality, sex, gender identity, sexual orientation, religion, geography, disability, age, and individual aspects such as personality, learning styles, and life experiences. Let's look at diversity through the lens of available AAMC data and other information.

- **First, consider race and ethnicity.** While diversity extends beyond this particular characteristic, it remains a critical component. The data show, for example, that only 7.1 percent of applicants are black or African-American, 5.9 percent are Hispanic or Latino, and 0.2 percent are American Indian or Alaska Native. (See Figure 4.1.)

- **What about family income?** This is another area of great imbalance. Parental income of students entering medical school skews heavily to the upper range, with a median income of $120,000. (That's almost double the estimated U.S. median family income of $52,100 reported by the U.S. Census Bureau.) Looking at it from another angle, almost one in six students comes from a home in which their parents earn $250,000 or more a year. (See Figure 4.2.)

- **Another perspective—gender.** On the surface, it appears that male and female applicants are fairly equal in number, but there are instances where that's not the case. You'll see, for example, in Figure 4.1 that there is a relative shortage of male black or African-American applicants. The AAMC recently published "Altering the Course: Black Males in Medicine" to better understand this trend and explore solutions (*www.aamc .org/blackmalesinmed*).

- **Benefits of diversity extend beyond education.** Increased diversity brings with it benefits that extend beyond the classroom. Research has shown that diversity in the physician workforce contributes to increased access to health care. Diversity among clinician scientists has been linked to an increase in research dedicated to diseases that disproportionately affect racial and ethnic minorities.

Figure 4.1. Applicants to U.S. medical schools, by race, ethnicity, and sex, 2014.

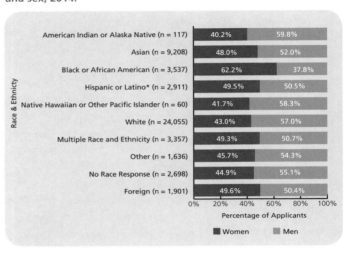

*Six students did not report sex so they were excluded here.
Source: AAMC Data Warehouse: Applicant Matriculant File, as of March 26, 2015.*

Figure 4.2. Parental income of entering medical students, 2015.

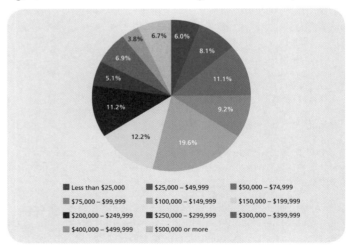

Source: AAMC's 2015 Matriculating Student Questionnaire (MSQ).

AAMC Programs and Resources

The AAMC is strongly committed to improving health for all. Considering the benefits that diversity offers, the AAMC is engaged in a number of programs and initiatives designed to help increase diversity to include all capable and promising students from a broad range of backgrounds. While these programs are open to all students, they are sensitive to the challenges and needs of individuals from groups underrepresented in medicine. These initiatives are described below.

Career Fairs and Enrichment Programs

Medical schools throughout the country provide various programs and resources designed to recruit students and prepare them for medical education. Some of these programs are held during the school year, others in the summer. They are designed for high school students, college students, and those who already have completed undergraduate study.

The AAMC is affiliated with two such programs:

- **Minority Student Medical Career Awareness Workshops and Recruitment Fair.** This event is typically held each fall in conjunction with Learn Serve Lead: The AAMC Annual Meeting. Students are encouraged to come and explore the possibilities in medicine. College and high school students, parents, pre-health advisors, school administrators, and any others interested in pursuing a career in medicine can meet diversity affairs and admission officers from U.S. medical schools and other health professions schools to discuss medical school preparation, enrichment programs, admission policies and procedures, financial aid, and more. Attendees can also participate in interactive medical and health activities and workshops. The AAMC also hosts other career fairs in conjunction with meetings for student affairs and graduate education. Information about these events is available at *www.aamc.org/medicalcareerfair*.

- **Summer Medical and Dental Education Program (SMDEP).** The Robert Wood Johnson Foundation's Summer Medical and Dental Education Program is a free, six-week academic enrichment program for college freshmen and sophomores interested in careers in medicine or dentistry. Components of the program include science- and mathematics-based courses, learning and study skills seminars, career development activities, clinical experiences, and a financial planning workshop. Funded by the Robert Wood Johnson Foundation and offered at 12 U.S. medical and 9 dental schools across the nation, the program includes a stipend, housing, and meals. For additional information, visit *www.smdep.org* or call, toll free, 1-866-58-SMDEP.

Aspiring Docs—An AAMC Resource to Increase Diversity in Medicine

Having a diverse workforce of doctors is essential to providing the best care for all communities and improving the health of all.

The AAMC's Aspiring Docs website provides resources and inspiration to help you get started on your path to medicine. The website includes inspiring stories from medical students and doctors about how they overcame challenges, videos of medical students answering questions from applicants, and one-page fact sheets to help you get started as you prepare to apply. To see what other applicants are saying about being a pre-med, and to read what medical students and residents are doing every day, follow the Aspiring Docs Diaries blog (*aspiringdocsdiaries.org*). You can even email *aspiringdocs@aamc.org* if you'd like to submit a blog post!

Aspiring Docs offers the most reliable tools and information to anyone considering a career in medicine. To access the growing library of information and resources, visit *www.aamc.org/aspiringdocs*.

Additional AAMC Resources

The AAMC also offers a wide variety of publications, online tools, and other information at the Minorities in Medicine website at *www.aamc.org/students/minorities* and the Diversity and Inclusion website at *www.aamc.org/diversity*. Among the resources you will find are:

Medical Students with Disabilities: Resources to Enhance Accessibility. This recently published guide informs users about current resources available to medical schools as they accept and matriculate a growing number of medical students with a wide range of disabilities. Specifically, there is an emphasis in this publication on the assistive technologies available for medical students. You can order a copy of this guide at *members.aamc.org/eweb/DynamicPage.aspx?webcode=PubHome*.

Enrichment Programs Online. This site includes a free database to help students locate summer enrichment programs on medical school campuses. You can search by school, state, region, area of focus, and length of program. Go to *services.aamc.org/summerprograms* to explore programs of interest.

Medical Minority Applicant Registry (Med-MAR). During the MCAT registration, students who are either economically disadvantaged or from racial and ethnic groups that are historically underrepresented in medicine can select the Medical Minority Applicant Registry (Med-MAR) option to be included in the registry. This Web-based program provides medical schools with basic biographical information and MCAT scores of registered examinees, thereby giving institutions opportunities to enhance their diversity efforts. Go to *www.aamc.org/medmar* for more information.

For information about the definition of "underrepresented" in medicine, visit *www.aamc.org/urm*.

Fee Assistance Program. The AAMC believes that the cost of applying to medical school should not be an insurmountable barrier and offers a Fee Assistance Program, which is available to students whose financial limitations would otherwise prevent them from taking the MCAT exam or applying to medical school. Details about the Fee Assistance Program can be found at *www.aamc.org/students/applying/fap* and in Chapter 7 of this book.

Data About Applicants, Matriculants, and Graduates. The AAMC also collects and presents detailed data about medical students from different racial and ethnic groups, most of which are available online free of charge on the AAMC website (and a good deal of which are included in this guide). (See also Table 4.1 at the end of this chapter.) Several resources are likely to be of interest:

- A large collection of data about medical school applicants, matriculants, and graduates is available on the AAMC website at *www.aamc.org/facts*.

- The AAMC publication *Diversity in Medical Education, Facts & Figures 2014* provides race and ethnicity data on medical school applicants, accepted applicants, matriculants, enrollment, graduates, and faculty. You can access the full text without charge at *aamcdiversityfactsandfigures.org*.

- Data on medical school faculty, including information by self-identification, can be found at *www.aamc.org/data/facultyroster/reports*.

School Programs and Resources

Just as the AAMC is committed to the issue of diversity, colleges and medical schools are also invested in making medical education accessible to all. Take some time to explore the resources on the next page as well.

Premedical School Programs at Undergraduate Colleges. Pre-health advisors have an abundance of information and data at their fingertips. Not only can they help you with the application process and refer you to appropriate contacts, they also know about programs that students from underrepresented groups and disadvantaged backgrounds have found useful. If your college has a pre-health advisor (and the majority of them do), make sure you take advantage of this valuable resource. To learn more about pre-health advisors or to locate one if your school doesn't have an advising office, visit *www.naahp.org*.

Medical School Websites. In addition to the individual profiles in the Medical School Admission Requirements website, you'll want to explore the medical school websites for information on their diversity programs and resources. Go to *www.aamc.org/medicalschools* for a listing of all U.S. and Canadian MD-granting medical schools and links to their websites.

Medical School Diversity Affairs Representatives. Other invaluable resources are medical school diversity affairs representatives. These individuals are dedicated to increasing diversity among medical schools at their institutions and are an excellent source of information for applicants (or potential applicants). You can get the name of the diversity affairs contacts at any U.S. medical school through the Directory of Diversity Affairs Representatives database. It's searchable by name, location, and institution, and it's available at *www.aamc.org/members/ gsa/committees_gsa/coda/55126/cosda_welcome .html*. Contact information is also available within each medical school profile on the Medical School Admission Requirements website at *www.aamc.org/msar*.

Financial Assistance for Medical School. Don't let the cost of medical school deter you from your dreams. As you'll learn in Chapter 10, more than four-fifths of medical students across the country receive some form of financial assistance. Medical schools—both public and private—work hard to offer a variety of financial aid plans to ensure that capable students are not denied access to their institutions because of financial limitations. In addition to discussing possibilities for assistance with the financial aid officer at the medical schools that interest you, you should familiarize yourself with general information about financing a medical education by reading the relevant material in this book and reviewing the wealth of information about loans (and other programs) at *www.aamc.org/ first*.

Programs at Medical Schools. Once you've enrolled in medical school, you'll find that a variety of academic and personal support programs is available to you. These programs help students from various backgrounds to successfully complete their medical studies, with the ultimate goal of increasing diversity among physicians entering careers in patient care, teaching, and research and eliminating racial and ethnic disparities in health care.

For those who wish to explore the benefits of diversity, we suggest the following readings:

Antonio AL, Chang MJ, Hakuta K, Kenny DA, Levin S, Milem JF. Effects of racial diversity on complex thinking in college students. *Psychological Science*. 2004, 15:507–510.

Denson N, Chang M. Racial diversity matters: The impact of diversity-related student engagement and institutional context. *American Educational Research Journal*. 2009, 46(2):322–353.

Gurin P. The compelling need for diversity in higher education: Expert testimony in Gratz, et al. v. Bollinger, et al. Michigan *Journal of Race and Law*. 1999, 5:363–425.

Saha S, Guiton G, Wimmers PF, Wilkerson L. Student body racial and ethnic composition and diversity-related outcomes in US medical schools. *JAMA*. 2008, 300:1135–1145.

Smith DG. *Diversity's Promise for Higher Education: Making It Work*. Baltimore, MD: The Johns Hopkins University Press, 2009.

Smith DG and Associates. *Diversity Works: The Emerging Picture of How Students Benefit*. Washington, DC: Association of American Colleges and Universities, 1997.

Whitla DK, Orfield G, Silen W, Teperow C, Howard C, Reede J. Educational benefit of diversity in medical school: A survey of students. *Academic Medicine*. 2003, 78:460–466.

No Advisor? Contact the NAAHP for Help

If your institution does not have a pre-health advisor, you can contact the **National Association of Advisors for the Health Professions** (NAAHP). There, you'll find a list of NAAHP members who have volunteered to help students without access to a pre-health advisor from a distance. Learn more about what pre-health advisors do and how to locate one at *www.naahp.org/StudentResources/ FindanAdvisor.aspx*.

Table 4.1. Matriculants, by Medical School, Race, and Ethnicity, 2015*

State	School	Hispanic or Latino	Asian	Black	Native American**	Native Hawaiian/OPI	White	Other	Unduplicated Total
AL	Alabama	6	22	4	7	1	143	6	186
AL	South Alabama	2	14	0	8	0	49	3	75
AR	Arkansas	4	19	4	7	0	138	2	171
AZ	Arizona	26	18	11	7	0	63	3	117
AZ	Arizona Phoenix	9	19	0	2	0	45	7	80
CA	California Northstate	2	26	0	2	0	25	5	60
CA	Loma Linda	18	53	3	13	1	74	3	169
CA	Southern Cal-Keck	14	64	2	17	0	78	8	184
CA	Stanford	12	34	2	6	0	39	2	90
CA	UC Berkeley/SF Joint Program	1	7	0	2	0	9	0	16
CA	UC Davis	26	37	0	12	2	29	13	110
CA	UC Irvine	14	37	0	5	0	42	6	104
CA	UC Riverside	14	15	1	7	0	13	7	50
CA	UC San Diego	12	42	1	11	2	63	5	125
CA	UC San Francisco	25	45	1	19	0	71	4	149
CA	UCLA Drew	10	1	0	12	1	0	0	24
CA	UCLA-Geffen	24	65	1	10	1	44	6	151
CO	Colorado	24	39	5	6	1	109	5	180
CT	Connecticut	9	19	2	13	0	58	2	99
CT	Quinnipiac-Netter	8	22	0	2	0	48	5	91
CT	Yale	15	34	2	6	1	43	3	104
DC	George Washington	19	41	0	19	2	92	8	179
DC	Georgetown	9	29	2	11	1	137	9	196
DC	Howard	11	18	0	73	0	6	5	117
FL	FIU-Wertheim	44	20	2	14	0	53	7	123
FL	Florida	15	18	3	16	1	83	5	135
FL	Florida Atlantic-Schmidt	7	11	0	5	0	40	2	64
FL	Florida State	29	10	4	11	0	67	4	120
FL	Miami-Miller	24	53	0	11	2	109	5	197
FL	UCF	10	46	0	3	1	58	5	121
FL	USF-Morsani	6	57	1	12	3	91	11	177
GA	Emory	2	20	0	11	0	88	4	135
GA	GRU MC Georgia	23	52	1	39	0	119	11	230
GA	Mercer	4	15	0	3	0	82	4	108
GA	Morehouse	7	6	2	64	0	9	3	84
HI	Hawaii-Burns	1	52	1	0	15	17	2	68
IA	Iowa-Carver	9	28	0	3	0	107	5	152
IL	Chicago Med Franklin	15	51	1	14	0	99	18	190
IL	Chicago-Pritzker	6	21	0	11	2	45	4	88
IL	Illinois	51	71	3	37	0	151	12	315
IL	Loyola-Stritch	14	39	3	7	0	77	5	159
IL	Northwestern-Feinberg	19	58	1	9	3	72	7	164
IL	Rush	8	27	0	5	0	83	7	128
IL	Southern Illinois	4	9	0	6	0	53	2	72
IN	Indiana	34	56	3	38	0	231	12	355
KS	Kansas	12	26	2	12	0	154	9	211
KY	Kentucky	2	13	0	8	0	101	3	137
KY	Louisville	5	18	0	9	0	118	5	154
LA	LSU New Orleans	7	15	4	13	0	150	6	194
LA	LSU Shreveport	5	11	0	5	0	102	4	124
LA	Tulane	5	45	1	5	1	120	8	181
MA	Boston	19	54	0	7	2	82	4	180
MA	Harvard	17	52	0	11	0	77	6	165
MA	Massachusetts	4	27	0	7	0	76	5	125
MA	Tufts	18	36	0	9	0	134	9	201
MD	Johns Hopkins	7	38	0	10	0	56	3	120
MD	Maryland	8	44	0	7	1	92	5	159
MD	Uniformed Services-Hebert	11	32	0	9	2	118	4	170
MI	Central Michigan	8	8	1	6	0	69	6	104
MI	Michigan	16	39	2	10	0	108	9	170

(continued)

State	School	Hispanic or Latino	Asian	Black	Native American**	Native Hawaiian/OPI	White	Other	Unduplicated Total
MI	Michigan State	16	38	0	15	1	109	10	189
MI	Oakland Beaumont	4	37	0	3	0	65	7	125
MI	Wayne State	5	62	0	10	0	168	12	290
MI	Western Michigan-Stryker	8	14	1	1	0	32	3	60
MN	Mayo	4	12	1	3	0	31	3	53
MN	Minnesota	14	29	10	14	0	169	7	230
MO	Missouri Columbia	4	16	0	2	0	80	7	104
MO	Missouri Kansas City	1	46	3	12	0	43	0	106
MO	Saint Louis	1	54	0	10	0	103	1	181
MO	Washington U St Louis	10	32	1	4	1	69	3	123
MS	Mississippi	2	15	1	15	0	109	3	145
NC	Duke	7	30	0	13	1	57	6	115
NC	East Carolina-Brody	2	14	2	8	0	58	1	80
NC	North Carolina	13	30	3	23	0	113	5	181
NC	Wake Forest	3	19	0	13	0	79	7	120
ND	North Dakota	2	3	7	0	0	71	1	78
NE	Creighton	6	31	1	3	0	115	3	157
NE	Nebraska	1	13	0	1	0	109	0	127
NH	Dartmouth-Geisel	10	20	2	11	1	41	2	92
NJ	Cooper Rowan	6	18	0	7	0	53	2	79
NJ	Rutgers New Jersey	22	76	0	8	0	65	8	178
NJ	Rutgers-RW Johnson	18	59	0	12	0	90	8	190
NM	New Mexico	36	12	6	4	0	52	5	103
NV	Nevada	5	17	2	2	0	47	1	70
NY	Albany	8	43	0	11	1	71	9	137
NY	Buffalo-Jacobs	14	21	0	9	0	100	4	144
NY	Columbia	18	38	0	22	1	78	6	159
NY	Cornell-Weill	12	28	0	7	0	52	4	106
NY	Einstein	12	40	0	11	0	106	4	183
NY	Hofstra North Shore-LIJ	14	26	0	4	0	58	4	99
NY	Mount Sinai-Icahn	9	38	0	13	0	65	8	140
NY	New York Medical	23	38	2	31	0	101	5	202
NY	New York University	24	30	2	16	0	61	7	132
NY	Rochester	6	23	0	13	0	56	1	104
NY	SUNY Downstate	9	78	0	14	0	79	9	189
NY	SUNY Upstate	10	27	0	13	0	97	5	159
NY	Stony Brook	10	46	1	8	0	54	5	132
OH	Case Western Reserve	10	72	3	14	0	98	8	216
OH	Cincinnati	12	33	0	10	1	111	6	174
OH	Northeast Ohio	3	56	1	5	0	73	13	147
OH	Ohio State	17	47	2	23	0	101	6	191
OH	Toledo	1	36	0	12	0	112	13	177
OH	Wright State-Boonshoft	7	18	1	15	0	64	6	111
OK	Oklahoma	5	22	16	3	0	132	3	161
OR	Oregon	7	24	1	3	1	101	4	146
PA	Commonwealth	9	14	3	7	0	72	2	105
PA	Drexel	10	88	2	15	0	131	8	261
PA	Jefferson-Kimmel	17	51	2	7	1	174	11	267
PA	Penn State	10	37	0	4	0	95	3	149
PA	Pennsylvania-Perelman	26	39	0	11	0	77	4	156
PA	Pittsburgh	7	35	2	11	0	86	4	148
PA	Temple	20	44	3	13	4	126	4	205
PR	Caribe	63	1	1	0	0	11	1	67
PR	Ponce	66	4	0	1	0	13	1	76
PR	Puerto Rico	108	0	0	3	0	6	0	110
PR	San Juan Bautista	51	4	0	1	0	11	0	63
RI	Brown-Alpert	16	40	0	13	0	70	6	144
SC	MU South Carolina	7	22	2	24	1	119	3	176
SC	South Carolina	1	10	0	7	0	69	3	94
SC	South Carolina Greenville	3	12	0	7	0	79	3	99

(continued)

Table 4.1. Matriculants, by Medical School, Race, and Ethnicity, 2015* *(continued)*

State	School	Hispanic or Latino	Asian	Black	Native American**	Native Hawaiian/OPI	White	Other	Unduplicated Total
SD	South Dakota-Sanford	1	0	2	0	0	68	0	70
TN	East Tennessee-Quillen	3	6	1	5	0	56	1	72
TN	Meharry	7	4	2	85	1	10	3	105
TN	Tennessee	5	23	4	20	0	106	7	165
TN	Vanderbilt	8	12	4	3	1	60	3	90
TX	Baylor	22	67	0	11	0	89	2	185
TX	Texas A & M	27	62	1	6	0	102	5	198
TX	Texas Tech	23	52	1	9	0	94	3	180
TX	Texas Tech-Foster	24	25	1	4	0	54	2	104
TX	UT HSC San Antonio	42	41	5	15	1	130	0	210
TX	UT Houston	24	81	1	11	1	128	9	240
TX	UT Medical Branch	50	52	1	18	0	123	5	230
TX	UT Southwestern	23	97	1	13	0	92	1	232
UT	Utah	4	19	1	1	0	89	6	122
VA	Eastern Virginia	9	39	1	6	0	100	5	151
VA	Virginia	14	27	1	18	1	79	4	156
VA	Virginia Commonwealth	16	66	1	11	1	116	5	216
VA	Virginia Tech Carilion	3	16	0	3	0	21	2	42
VT	Vermont	11	19	0	4	0	78	4	114
WA	U Washington	8	41	5	5	0	192	5	245
WI	MC Wisconsin	11	34	0	16	1	162	5	230
WI	Wisconsin	7	32	2	5	1	129	3	176
WV	Marshall-Edwards	3	6	0	5	1	59	5	75
WV	West Virginia	8	16	0	3	0	84	2	110

*Data are not reflective of the number of individuals in each demographic category, but rather the number of times a particular race or ethnic category was selected. One individual can self-identify with multiple groups.
**Including Alaska native.
Source: AAMC Data Warehouse: Applicant and Matriculant File as of October 19, 2015.

Worksheets at the end of chapters in this guide are available in fillable PDF format at www.aamc.org/msar-resources.

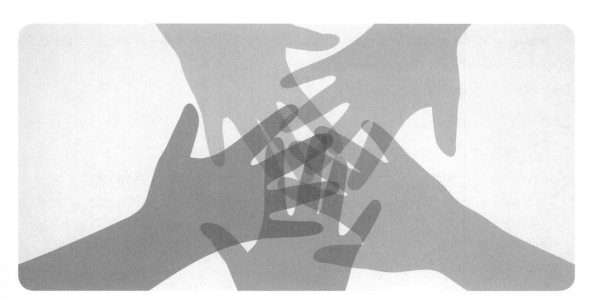

Use this worksheet to identify programs you may be eligible for. Many programs primarily sponsored by medical schools are available to students across the United States. You can start searching at *services.aamc .org/summerprograms* and *ExploreHealthCareers.org*, and then use this worksheet to figure out your options.

Before the Application Process

For example: Summer Medical and Dental Education Program (SMDEP)

- Description: Six-week academic enrichment program that offers students both academic and career experiences that will support their dental or medical school career preparation. For more Information, go to *smdep.org*.

- Eligibility: _____

- Which academic year(s) would I be eligible to participate?: _____

- When am I eligible to apply?: _____ • Application deadline: _____

- Accepts out-of-state?: ❏ Yes ❏ No ❏ Other: _____

During the Application Process

For example: Medical Minority Applicant Registry (Med-MAR)

- Description: During the MCAT registration, students who are either economically disadvantaged or from racial and ethnic groups that are historically underrepresented in medicine can select the Medical Minority Applicant Registry (Med-MAR). This Web-based program provides medical schools with basic biographical information and MCAT scores of registered examinees, thereby giving them opportunities to enhance their diversity efforts. For more information, go to *www.aamc.org/medmar*.

- Eligibility: _____

- Which academic year(s) would I be eligible to participate?: _____

- When am I eligible to apply?: _____ • Application deadline: _____

- Accepts out-of-state? ❏ Yes ❏ No ❏ Other: _____

During the Application Process

Program: _____

- Description: _____

  _____

- Eligibility: _____

- Which academic year(s) would I be eligible to participate?: _____

- When am I eligible to apply?: _____ • Application deadline: _____

- Accepts out-of-state? ❏ Yes ❏ No ❏ Other: _____

Chapter 5

All About the MCAT® Exam

After my third attempt applying to medical school, I was ready to give up. With my husband's encouragement, I prepared for my fourth and final application, no matter the outcome. Being several years beyond college, I was apprehensive about taking the exam, but I was hopeful that if I studied enough, I could earn a higher score and make myself a more competitive candidate.

While I waited to reapply, I kept doing things that were important to me, such as working in a research lab and volunteering with hospice patients. During that time, I also earned a master of bioethics and medical humanities degree. All of these things were worth the time I invested, as they became major topics of interest during my interviews.

Allison Lyle, MA
MD Candidate
University of Louisville School of
Medicine
Class of 2017

On the morning of my test, I was embarrassed to be taking this exam again, but I was comforted to find that several of my fellow examinees were also retaking the exam. Taking the exam more than once is not recommended for everyone. In my case, thankfully, this exam went well, and I am now a third-year medical student.

The Role of the MCAT Exam

Simply put, the MCAT exam helps admission officers identify which students are likely to succeed in medical school. That's done by spotting those students who not only have a basic knowledge of the natural, behavioral, and social sciences, which provides the foundation necessary in the early years of medical school, but also those with strong critical analysis and reasoning skills.

One can argue that college grades essentially do the same thing. But because an "A" in one school is not necessarily equivalent to an "A" in another, admission officers don't have a "standard measure" against which to evaluate students. The MCAT exam fills that void. As a result, virtually every medical school in the United States, and many in Canada, requires applicants to submit recent MCAT scores.

Admission officers look at MCAT scores in conjunction with your grades and with many other selection factors, including those related to your experiences and personal attributes, when making their decisions.

Using all these components, medical school admission committees are able to substantially increase their success in predicting who will be successful in medical school.

These application programs and institutions use MCAT scores:

- American Medical College Application Service® (AMCAS®)
- American Association of Colleges of Osteopathic Medicine Application Service (AACOMAS®)
- Texas Medical and Dental Schools Application Service (TMDSAS)
- Ontario Medical School Application Service (OMSAS)
- Other Canadian medical schools requiring MCAT scores
- American Association of Colleges of Podiatric Medicine Application Service (AACPM)
- Veterinary Medical College Application Service (VMCAS)
- Schools of Public Health Application Service (SOPHAS)

How the Exam Is Structured

There are four test sections:

- Biological and Biochemical Foundations of Living Systems
- Chemical and Physical Foundations of Biological Systems
- Psychological, Social, and Biological Foundations of Behavior
- Critical Analysis and Reasoning Skills

Three sections of the test are organized around foundational concepts in the natural, behavioral, and social sciences. They reflect current research about the most effective ways for students to learn and use science, emphasizing deep knowledge of the most important scientific concepts over knowledge simply of many discrete scientific facts.

Science education leaders say that some of the most important foundational concepts in the sciences ask students to integrate and analyze information from different disciplines. In that vein, questions in these sections will ask you to combine your scientific knowledge from multiple disciplines with your scientific inquiry and reasoning skills. You'll be asked to demonstrate four different scientific inquiry and reasoning skills on the exam:

- Knowledge of scientific concepts and principles
- Scientific reasoning and problem solving
- Reasoning about the design and execution of research
- Data-based and statistical reasoning

The fourth section, Critical Analysis and Reasoning Skills, will be similar to many of the verbal reasoning tests you've taken in your academic career. It includes passages and questions that test your ability to comprehend and analyze what you read. This section asks you to read and think about passages from a wide range of disciplines in the social sciences and humanities, including population health, ethics and philosophy, and studies of diverse cultures. Passages are followed by a series of questions that lead you through the process of comprehending, analyzing, and reasoning about the material you've read. This section was developed specifically to measure the analytical and reasoning skills you'll need to be successful in medical school.

What the Exam Measures

The different sections of the MCAT exam are carefully designed to test the concepts and skills most needed by entering medical students.

The Biological and Biochemical Foundations of Living Systems and the Chemical and Physical Foundations of Biological Systems sections are designed to:

- Test introductory-level biology, organic and inorganic chemistry, and physics concepts taught in year-long courses

- Test biochemistry concepts at the level taught in many colleges and universities in first-semester biochemistry courses

- Test cellular and molecular biology topics at the level taught in many colleges and universities in introductory biology sequences and first-semester biochemistry courses

- Target basic research methods and statistics concepts described by many baccalaureate faculty as important to success in introductory science courses

- Have you demonstrate your scientific inquiry and reasoning, research methods, and statistics skills, as applied to the natural sciences

The Psychological, Social, and Biological Foundations of Behavior section is designed to:

- Test your knowledge and use of the concepts in psychology, sociology, and biology that provide a solid foundation for learning about the behavioral and sociocultural determinants of health in medical school

- Target concepts taught at many colleges and universities in first-semester psychology and sociology courses

- Target biology concepts that relate to mental processes and behavior that are taught at many colleges and universities in introductory biology

- Target basic research methods and statistics concepts described by many baccalaureate faculty as important to success in introductory science courses and described in many introductory psychology and sociology courses

- Have you demonstrate your scientific inquiry and reasoning, research methods, and statistics skills, as applied to the social and behavioral sciences

The Critical Analysis and Reasoning Skills section is designed to:

- Test your comprehension, analysis, and reasoning skills by asking you to critically analyze information provided in reading passages

- Include content from ethics, philosophy, studies of diverse cultures, population health, and a wide range of social sciences and humanities disciplines

- Provide all the information you need to answer questions in the passages

MCAT Scores

You'll receive five results from your MCAT exam: one for each of the four sections and one combined, total score. The MCAT exam is not graded on a curve. Below is the information you'll receive in your score report.

Section Scores

Each of the four sections—Biological and Biochemical Foundations of Living Systems; Chemical and Physical Foundations of Biological Systems; Psychological, Social, and Biological Foundations of Behavior; and Critical Analysis and Reasoning Skills—is scored from a low of 118 to a high of 132, with a midpoint of 125. You'll receive a score for each of the four sections. (See the sample score report in Figure 5.1.)

Total Score

Your scores for the four sections are combined to create your total score. The total score ranges from 472 to 528. The midpoint is 500.

For example, if you scored 127 on the Biological and Biochemical Foundations of Living Systems section; 124 on the Chemical and Physical Foundations of Biological Systems section; 127 on the Psychological, Social, and Biological Foundations of Behavior section; and 123 on the Critical Analysis and Reasoning Skills section, your total score would be 501.

Figure 5.1. Sample MCAT score report.

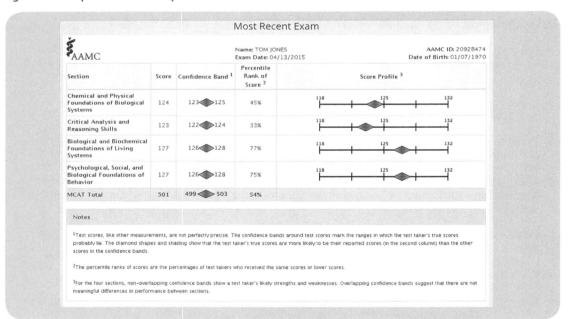

Percentile Ranks

The percentile ranks show how you scored relative to other MCAT examinees. You'll receive percentile ranks for each individual section score and for your overall total score. Each percentile rank represents the percentage of examinees with a score at or below your score, and scores with higher percentile ranks represent higher levels of performance on the exam.

Confidence Bands

Like other standardized tests, the MCAT exam is an imperfect measure of what test takers know and can do. Examinees' scores can be affected by factors like fatigue, test anxiety, and less-than-optimal test-room conditions. But then again, an examinee's score might be boosted if they were recently exposed to some of the topics included on the exam. The inclusion of the new confidence bands is meant to remind admission officers not to overemphasize small differences in test scores.

Score Profiles

Score profiles are included to show your strengths and weaknesses across the four sections of the exam. This section of the score report can help you determine how to focus your preparation if you decide to retake the exam.

You can learn more about the score scale and score report at *www.aamc.org/students/applying/mcat/scores*.

Valid MCAT Scores

Each medical school sets its own policy about how much time can elapse between when you take the exam and when you apply, and about the latest date of an exam it will accept during the application cycle. To find out the acceptable timing for the schools you're interested in, contact them directly or visit the Medical School Admission Requirements website, where there's a table showing which schools are accepting scores from the previous exam in their admission cycles: *www.aamc.org/msar*.

International Students

If you are an international student, you are welcome to take the MCAT exam, provided that you meet the eligibility requirements described. If you are in an MBBS (Bachelor of Medicine/Bachelor of Surgery) degree program or hold the MBBS degree, you may register for the MCAT exam without seeking special permission.

Scores from the New MCAT Exam

Students began taking the new MCAT exam in April 2015. While data are not yet available for applicants who were accepted to and enrolled in medical school for 2016, Figures 5.2–5.6 provide information (from the AAMC Data Warehouse) about those who applied for 2016 admission with scores from the new MCAT exam. Because the 2016 application cycle had not closed at the time of the publication, the data should be considered preliminary; they are current as of January 11, 2016. Figure 5.2 shows the percentage of examinees and applicants achieving a specific total score.

Figures 5.3 through 5.6 summarize the scores of people who took the new exam in 2015 and of applicants who submitted new scores in the 2016 application cycle. Each graph shows the percentage of examinees and applicants achieving a specific score for each section of the test.

Figure 5.2. Percentage of 2015 MCAT examinees and of 2016 medical school applicants, by MCAT total score.

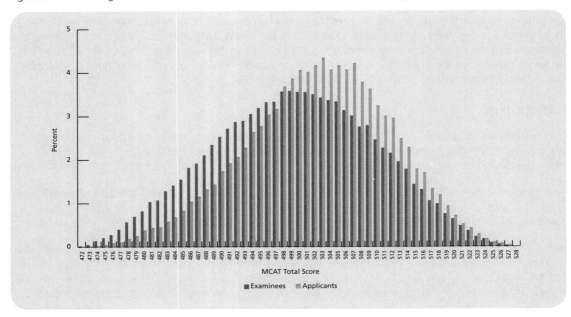

Figure 5.3. Percentage of 2015 MCAT examinees and of 2016 medical school applicants, by Biological and Biochemical Foundations of Living Systems section score.

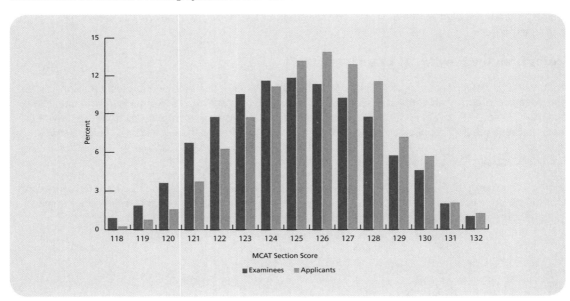

Figure 5.4. Percentage of 2015 MCAT examinees and of 2016 medical school applicants, by Chemical and Physical Foundations of Biological Systems section score.

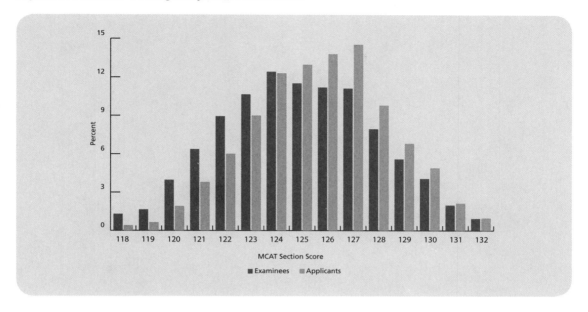

Figure 5.5. Percentage of 2015 MCAT examinees and of 2016 medical school applicants, by Psychological, Social, and Biological Foundations of Behavior section score.

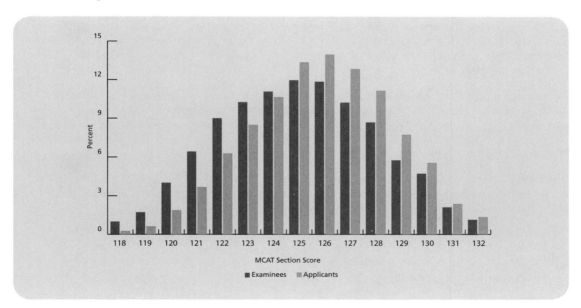

Figure 5.6. Percentage of 2015 MCAT examinees and of 2016 medical school applicants, by Critical Analysis and Reasoning Skills section score.

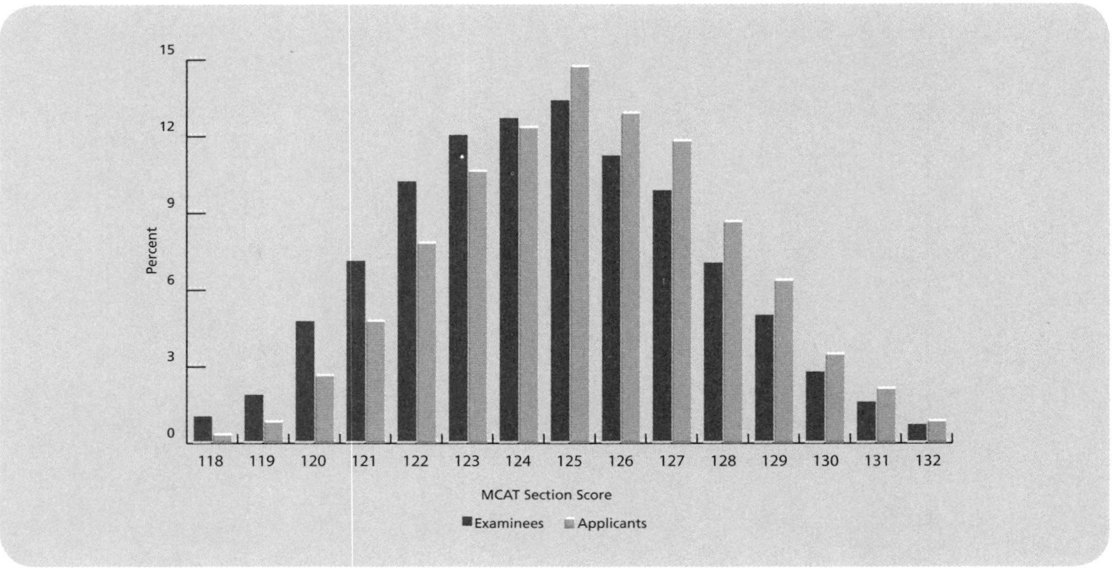

Preparing for the Exam

While there's no one way to prepare for the MCAT exam, making sure you give yourself adequate time to prepare is critical. The amount of time you'll need really depends on you. Have you completed all the coursework that is associated with the content on the exam? Do you feel confident in all content areas? Are there some content topics or skills that you feel require more in-depth study or practice? Are you comfortable with the online testing format?

You may find it useful to break down studying into manageable chunks, realizing that you can't tackle everything at once. This will also help give you a sense of the amount of time you'll need so you can prepare at a comfortable pace. The best study plans are those that are tailored to an individual's needs.

To understand what's on the exam:

- Review this interactive content tool: **What's on the MCAT exam?** (*www.aamc.org/mcat2015exam*). It offers an overview of the exam sections, in both video and text format, as well as details about foundational concepts and skills you'll be asked to demonstrate on the exam.

- See **The Official Guide to the MCAT Exam** (*www.aamc.org/officialmcatguide*), which is the first and only official comprehensive overview of the new exam. It includes 120 practice questions and solutions. The print book is available for purchase on the AAMC website and as an e-book through Amazon and Barnes & Noble.

- Visit *www.aamc.org/mcat* to read the **MCAT® Essentials**.

To study the content on the exam:

- Visit **Khan Academy's MCAT Collection**. More than 1,100 videos and 3,000 review questions are available, and the collection continues to grow. It was created in collaboration with the AAMC and the Robert Wood Johnson Foundation. Learn more at *khanacademy.org/test-prep/mcat*.

- Review the **Psychology and Sociology Textbook Roadmap**. Publishers of introductory psychology and sociology textbooks have provided in the roadmap detailed information on where in their textbooks to find the concepts you'll need for the new Psychological, Social, and Biological Foundations of Behavior section of the MCAT exam. Some of the textbooks in the roadmap are free, available online and in e-book format.

To practice for the exam: The AAMC has many official products, written by the test developers, to help you prepare for the exam, including a **Sample Test**, a **Practice Exam** with scaled scoring, a **Section Bank**, and **Question Packs**. Learn more at *www.aamc.org/mcat/preparing*.

Test Dates, Registration, and Fees

In 2016, the MCAT exam will be administered 20 times from January through September. (The dates are posted on the MCAT website, *www.aamc.org/mcat*.) Although the AAMC selects exam dates to ensure that scores are available to meet most medical school application deadlines, we recommend that you check the specific scheduling requirements of the schools of your choice, provided in the Medical School Admission Requirements website school profiles (*www.aamc.org/msar*). Once you've determined your preferred date, you can find the registration schedule for that particular exam session on the Registration Deadline Schedule, also posted online.

To be sure that you get the most complete and up-to-date information about the MCAT® exam, it is crucial that you read the **MCAT® Essentials** (available online at *www.aamc.org/mcat*) before you register for the exam. After you've read that, you can register online through the MCAT website. There's a $305 fee for the exam, a payment that covers both the cost of the test itself and the distribution of your scores. If you register late, make changes to your registration, and/or test at an international site, there are additional charges.

Consider taking the MCAT exam 12 to 18 months before your expected entry into medical school—but not before you have completed basic coursework and are comfortable with your knowledge of introductory-level biology, general and organic chemistry, and physics, as well as first-semester psychology and sociology and first-semester biochemistry. Many medical schools prefer that applicants take the exam in the spring because of the short time between the availability of late summer scores and school application deadlines. (Taking the exam in the spring also allows time for students to retake the test later in the summer, if necessary.)

Also keep in mind there are testing limits for the MCAT exam. You can take the exam up to three times in a single testing year, four times over two consecutive testing years, and seven times in your lifetime.

For more guidance on deciding when to take or retake the exam, please consult with your pre-health advisor.

The AAMC believes cost should not be a barrier to aspiring doctors. Therefore, the AAMC Fee Assistance Program helps qualifying examinees with MCAT registration fees, test preparation products, and other AAMC complimentary products and services. To use the Fee Assistance Program, you must be approved for the benefit before registering for the exam. The benefits are not retroactive; you won't be given a refund for any resources or fees incurred before you qualify. Learn whether you might qualify for Fee Assistance at *students-residents.aamc.org/applying-medical-school/applying-medical-school-process/fee-assistance-program*.

Testing with Accommodations

The AAMC is committed to giving all individuals an opportunity to demonstrate their proficiency on the MCAT exam, and that includes ensuring access to people with disabilities in accordance with relevant law.

If you have a disability or medical condition that you believe requires an adjustment to the standard testing conditions, we encourage you to apply for accommodated testing.

For information about application timeframes and types of documentation needed, as well as how to apply, please see *www.aamc.org/students/applying/mcat/accommodations*.

Retaking the Exam

If you're not happy with your performance on the MCAT exam, you have the option to take it again. But it's a tough decision.

There are times when a retake is well worth considering. Perhaps you discovered that your coursework or study didn't cover the topics as thoroughly as you needed them to. Or there's a large discrepancy between your grade in a subject and your score on a particular section. Or maybe you simply didn't feel well the day of the exam. In all these cases, your pre-health advisor may be of great help, and we recommend you discuss the issue with him or her.

Score Reporting

Your scores will be available in the MCAT Score Reporting System (SRS), accessible through the AAMC website at *www.aamc.org/mcat*. You have two options for sending your MCAT scores to medical schools:

- **Send your scores to the AMCAS® service:** The AMCAS® service is the American Medical College Application Service®, which most U.S. medical schools take part in and which you will use to manage sending your application to participating institutions. Your MCAT scores are automatically released to AMCAS. This means that you don't need to take any additional steps to insert your scores into your application, but it also means that you can't withhold any of your MCAT scores from your AMCAS application. You can view a list of participating schools at *www.aamc.org/amcas*. Read more about AMCAS in Chapter 7.

- **Send your scores to non-AMCAS schools:** Use this option, detailed in the MCAT Score Reporting System, to send your MCAT scores to non-AMCAS schools and programs.

Gap Year and Career Changers: Taking the MCAT Exam

If you plan on taking a gap year or are changing careers, you'll want to be thoughtful about preparing for the MCAT exam. Consider factors such as how well you know the content tested by the exam and when you would ideally want to begin medical school. This will help you figure out the best time to take the exam.

- **Know when you want to apply:** Many examinees consider taking their MCAT exam in the calendar year before the year they plan to enter medical school. For example, if you were applying in 2016 for entrance to medical school in 2017, you would take the exam in 2016. If you plan on taking a gap year, think about whether you want to take the exam before, during, or after the year, and build in time to prepare.

- **Mastering the content:** You are the best judge of how prepared you are. First, determine whether there's coursework you need to take or whether you need more time to study. Some applicants also need to take additional coursework, retake coursework that is several years old, or complete postbaccalaureate programs in order to meet application requirements. Consider this when choosing an exam date because the timeline may affect whether the exam will still be accepted by various medical schools.

- **Retesting and testing limits:** If you think you might need to test more than once in a calendar year, try to schedule an exam date early in the year. This will give you more time to receive your scores and prepare for a retest. Remember: you can take the exam only three times in a single testing year, four times over two consecutive testing years, and seven times in a lifetime.

If you've never taken the MCAT exam and you don't currently have a pre-health advisor to help you prepare, the **National Association of Advisors for the Health Professions** has volunteer advisors available. More information is at *www.naahp.org*.

 Worksheets at the end of chapters in this guide are available in fillable PDF format at *www.aamc.org/msar-resources*.

Worksheet 5.1
Getting Ready to Take the MCAT Exam Checklist

Ask yourself these questions when you're getting ready for the MCAT exam.

- Am I familiar with what will be on the exam?   ❑ Yes ❑ No ❑ Unsure
  (See what's on the exam: *www.aamc.org/mcat2015exam.*)

- If no or unsure, what content or sections am I unsure about? _____

- Have I allowed enough time to study and feel comfortable with my knowledge of the content on the exam?

    o Chemical and Physical Foundations of Biological Systems

        ❑ Yes ❑ No, I need more time ❑ Unsure

    o Biological and Biochemical Foundations of Living Systems

        ❑ Yes ❑ No, I need more time ❑ Unsure

    o Psychological, Social, and Biological Foundations of Behavior

        ❑ Yes ❑ No, I need more time ❑ Unsure

    o Critical Analysis and Reasoning Skills

        ❑ Yes ❑ No, I need more time ❑ Unsure

If you have areas where you need more study, check out the AAMC's preparation resources, which offer the opportunity to get familiar with the online testing environment. Also, consider forming a study group at your school or with other applicants who are preparing for the exam. Talk to your pre-health advisor about resources you may have on campus or through your institution.

- Am I within one to two calendar years of wanting to apply to medical school?

        ❑ Yes ❑ No ❑ Unsure

- Have I spoken with my pre-health advisor? Does he/she agree that I am ready?

        ❑ Yes ❑ No ❑ Unsure

- Have I applied to see if I qualify for the Fee Assistance Program?

        ❑ Yes ❑ No ❑ Unsure

- Do I feel prepared and ready to take the exam?

        ❑ Yes ❑ No ❑ Unsure

If you answered "no" to many of these questions, consult with your pre-health advisor about developing a plan to take the exam. See *www.aamc.org/mcat* for information about creating a study plan. When you're close to registering for a test date, be sure to read the MCAT Essentials for important information on scheduling, registration, test day policies, and scoring (*aamc-orange.global.ssl.fastly.net/production/media/filer_public/b9/c3/b9c382ef-5746-4da1-9265-ae570bb655e1/mcat_essentials_2016_-_final2.pdf*).

Chapter 6

Choosing Your Schools

Matthew Joy, MD
General Surgery Resident
Virginia Tech Carilion School of Medicine
Class of 2014

When researching medical schools, consider what kind of education experience you are seeking. Geographic location was an obvious consideration for me, but I also looked at class sizes, grading systems (pass-fail versus traditional), teaching styles (lecture hall versus small groups), research requirements, and locations for clinical rotations. In medical school, I've realized the importance of different learning environments. For example, some applicants desire smaller class sizes and small-group learning, some prefer more structure, and others may thrive when offered more freedom to direct the course of their own education.

Once you determine your preferences, make a list and compare schools based on the criteria that matter most to you. This is a great time to use the Medical School Admission Requirements website (www.aamc.org/msar), where you can sort and compare school profiles based on class size, requirements, and a myriad of other factors.

Finally, whenever you visit a school, ask about the things on your list to get the current student, faculty, and administration perspectives.

In this chapter, you will learn about some important factors to consider when choosing the school that's right for you.

The Overall Mission of the School

If you've seen one medical school … you've seen one medical school. Many of the differences among schools are obvious. Some schools are located on the East Coast, some on the West. Some are private; others, public. Some have a large entering class; others, small. And, as explained in Chapter 3, medical schools vary in the content of their courses, in the way they teach, and even in the way they grade and evaluate students.

These are all factors you'll want to consider as you narrow your selection, and we touch on them in the following pages. But the differences go even deeper, and at a very core level, medical schools have diverse missions and priorities. Because of these distinctions, what is significant to one school may be of only moderate importance to another, and these qualities naturally carry into the selection process.

Deciding where to apply requires that you become aware of the differences among schools, which is crucial, but it's also important to analyze yourself—your skills, experiences, career goals, and so forth—to identify the most appropriate matches. Take, for instance, an institution that places a strong emphasis on primary care. Is that the career path you intend to follow? If so, and especially if you can demonstrate your interest through extensive experience related to that area, you become a more attractive candidate on that basis alone.

That's one example. Other schools may be actively seeking students from specific geographic or rural areas. Others may be looking for students with a high potential for a research career. Still others may want to increase the number of doctors who plan to practice in their state (often a goal of public institutions). The differing missions among schools are reflected in their admission policies and standards.

If you need help with this self-analysis, think back to the various experiences you've had over the years. The ones you found especially rewarding or inspirational are likely to correlate with a specific area of interest and, by extension, a career goal.

Did you volunteer for two summers at a clinic in a **rural, underserved area**? Perhaps that's the direction you'd like to take your career in. If so, you'll want to seek out medical schools that place a high priority in that area.

Were the part-time jobs you had while doing research particularly gratifying? If you'd like to pursue a **research career**, look for schools that have a strong reputation in that area or are known for graduating a large percentage of medical students pursuing research careers.

There are other ways that speak to your interests and career goals. Did you spend your junior year tutoring freshmen and sophomores in entry-level biology or chemistry? Perhaps you'd like to join a **medical school faculty** and educate the next generation of physicians. If so, look for a medical school that has a relatively large percentage of graduates in teaching positions.

Once again, keep in mind that applying to medical school is a two-way street. While you're looking for a match, so are the schools. Your experiences will provide good insights for the admission officers and help them determine whether your interests and their missions are congruent. If you don't know which medical career path you want to pursue yet, that's okay. Aim to get as many rich and diverse experiences as possible so you will be a well-rounded applicant.

Kicking Off Your Research

There are several ways you can research schools to identify the ones that best match your own strengths, interests, and goals. Here are some factors to consider in making your selection:

- Research reputation and opportunities

- Community-based experience and opportunities

- Geographic location

- School's teaching methods

- Program of elective courses

- Faculty mentorship

- Ability of school to place students in particular residency programs

- Medical specialties

- Residency programs at hospitals affiliated with the school

The Medical School Admission Requirements website: Start your research with the medical school profiles on this site, *www.aamc.org/msar*. Here, each institution includes a clear mission statement and a description of its selection factors.

School websites and literature: You'll also want to review information provided by schools themselves. Although the specific content varies by school, each includes detailed material for prospective students.

Advisors: Your pre-health advisor or career counselor will be able to recommend specific schools likely to be a good "fit." These advisors have a lot of insight about the application process, so don't overlook this resource. Also, make sure you attend health career fairs to speak with admission staff from medical schools and participate in pre-med or pre-health student organizations.

The Educational Program

It's easy to get caught up in a specific region or location, or you may recognize the name of a prestigious school and want to go there simply because it sounds impressive. You'll want to consider all your options, though. As you weigh your decision, you'll also want to consider the differences among the educational programs themselves.

There's likely going to be a strong relationship between a school's mission and its **curriculum**. You'll be able to gauge whether an institution's objectives align with your interests by analyzing course requirements and electives programs. A medical school with a mission to graduate more primary care doctors may, for example, have a track that provides additional training in that area. A school that emphasizes research may require their students to write a thesis or devote an extended period of time to scholarly pursuits.

As you do your research, also consider what **teaching methods** you find most effective. Do you tend to do well with self-directed or participatory learning exercises, or do you prefer a learning environment with the more traditional, lecture-based style? Although most medical schools use an educational model that combines a variety of methods, every program adapts their own design. Are you looking for classes that promote small-group discussions and problem-based learning exercises? Or are you more comfortable with a traditional teaching approach? Eventually, these are great topics to discuss with current students, but a good starting point for your exploration is a school's website, as well as the AAMC's curriculum directory (*www.aamc.org/initiatives/cir*).

There are key differences among **grading systems**. Some institutions use a pass/fail system or an honors/pass/fail system, while others use letter grades. Some students have definite preferences, and if you're one of them, you may wish to consider a school's grading system as you narrow your selection.

There are many other factors you might want to think about. How will you be evaluated? At what point must students pass the first two steps of the United States Medical Licensing Examination® (USMLE®) before advancing in their education? What level of academic support is available? Is there a mentor system, for instance? What about cultural organizations and support services for minority and first-generation students—are they available? Questions such as these will undoubtedly enter into your final decision as you deliberate among offers.

How Do GPA and MCAT Scores Factor In?

Don't choose schools based solely on where you think your grades and MCAT scores will be accepted. While there's no question that your educational record is important and that admission officers seek candidates who are likely to succeed academically in their programs, it's important to realize that **academics alone do not predict who will become an effective physician, and admission officers know that all too well**.

The fact that there are many instances in which a "high-scoring" applicant is not accepted to a medical school—and in which an applicant with lower-than-average grades and scores is—tells you that admission officers must be looking at other factors.

Admission officers are taking a more holistic approach to evaluating applicants. Through this practice, admission officers assess candidates more broadly, looking not only at their "metrics" (GPA and MCAT scores) but also at their experiences and personal attributes.

You can read about the holistic approach to admission in Chapter 8, "The Admission Decision."

Attending Medical School in Your Home State

State residents enrolled in state-supported medical schools pay lower tuition than nonresidents. In addition, in-state residents are often given preference for admission (compared with out-of-state residents) for at least some of their spaces because the school receives state government support. With this in mind, you may want to give strong consideration to the public institutions in your state as you decide where to apply. Note that residency requirements are established by each state. Check with individual medical schools for policies regarding qualifying for in-state or residential status.

Nationally, 61 percent of 2014 matriculants attended schools in their home state.

International Students

There's only a small number of international students—those who are not U.S. citizens or permitted to reside permanently in this country—at U.S. medical schools. If you are an international applicant, know that private medical schools are more likely to accept international students than public schools, and that most medical schools require completion of premedical coursework at a U.S. college or university. For more information, see the Aspiring Docs fact sheet on applying as an international applicant at *www.aamc.org/ aspiringdocs*.

Public or Private?

You may also be deliberating between public and private institutions. Typically, the most cost-effective option is to consider a public medical school in the state where you live. (If you're from out of state, the cost differential between a public and a private school virtually disappears. See Table 10.1 in Chapter 10.) But don't automatically assume, even if you're interested in a state school near your home, that the private route will be more expensive under all circumstances. Some private institutions have large endowments that allow them to provide significant scholarship aid to qualifying students. These scholarships lower the "effective" tuition rate and permit those students to graduate with less educational debt than they would have if they had attended a public medical school in their home state.

Cost is only one consideration, though. Another element to be aware of when investigating the differences between private and public institutions is the school's mission—and how it might relate to your own aspirations and interests. Although all medical schools—public or private—have different missions, certain public institutions may have specific goals related to their state, such as increasing the supply of physicians. (If the school is in your home state and you'd like to live and work there after graduation, that will be a factor from both your perspective and the school's.) Other public institutions were founded by state legislators with an emphasis on the needs of a particular patient population—such as elder, rural, or underserved groups—which should enter into your evaluation if that objective corresponds to your own career intentions.

Additional Factors to Consider

There are many other factors that may be important to you as you search for a good "fit," including these:

Location. Perhaps you simply prefer a specific geographic region. Do you want to be close to family and friends? Do you prefer a warmer (or cooler) climate? Are you a fan of the East Coast … or the South … or the West? What about a bustling city environment versus a rural one? These factors play to your comfort level, and all are valid considerations. Beyond that, though, location can also relate to your career goals, as well as to a school's mission. If you hope to specialize in geriatrics, for example, a medical school located in an area with a higher-than-average proportion of older adults may be your best choice.

That's looking at it from your perspective. Consider, for a moment, the school's perspective. In some cases, a school may be seeking students from particular geographic regions in order to bolster its diversity, and you'll want to consider the impact—if any—that your own state residence might have on your application to medical schools in other areas. On the other hand, there are schools that look for local, in-state students who will continue to work and contribute to communities in that state. Review each school's mission statement to see what they're seeking in their applicants.

Size and Demographics. The size and demographics of the medical school—both in terms of its student body and its faculty—may be a consideration for you as well. The school entries in the Medical School Admission Requirements website contain data on the prior year's entering class, including the number of students by gender as well as by self-reported identification (*www.aamc.org/msar*).

Costs. Medical education is expensive, and the expenses associated with particular institutions will no doubt be a factor in your decision. You won't know what your actual costs will be (or the degree of assistance you will receive) until a school sends you a financial aid package in conjunction with its acceptance offer. Still, in looking through the school entries in the Medical School Admission Requirements website, you can get a general idea about the relative expenses of each institution, and you can take those numbers into consideration as you narrow your selection.

"Additional" doesn't mean less important. Figure 6.1 shows what matriculating students felt about specific factors in deciding which school to attend.

Special Regional Opportunities

Finally, you should be aware that some states without a public medical school participate in special interstate and regional agreements that give their residents access to a medical education. Currently, there are five interstate agreements:

- The Delaware Institute of Medical Information and Research

    dhss.delaware.gov/dhss/dhcc/dimer.html
    1-302-577-3240
    1-800-292-7935

- The Finance Authority of Maine's Access to Medical Education Program

    www.famemaine.com/fi
    1-800-228-3734

- University of Utah School of Medicine Idaho Contract

    medicine.utah.edu/admissions/begin/residency.php
    1-208-282-2475, *residency@sa.utah.edu*

Figure 6.1. Matriculating students' responses to this question: In choosing the medical school you now (or will) attend, how important were the following factors?

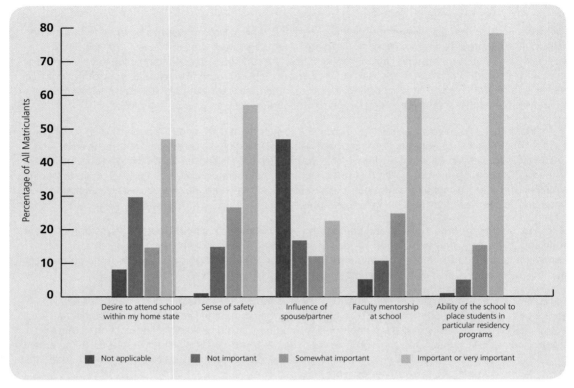

Source: AAMC's 2015 Matriculating Student Questionnaire (MSQ).

- The Western Interstate Commission for Higher Education

  www.wiche.edu/psep/medi
  1-303-541-0200

- The WWAMI (Washington, Wyoming, Alaska, Montana, and Idaho) Program

  uwmedicine.washington.edu/Education/WWAMI/Pages/Medical-School.aspx

You can learn more about each of these regional opportunities by visiting their websites or calling their program offices.

Worksheets at the end of chapters in this guide are available in fillable PDF format at *www.aamc.org/msar-resources*.

Worksheet 6.1
Factors to Weigh Before Applying

Use this form to identify and assess the schools where you may apply.

The Medical School Admission Requirement website allows you to filter your search for different medical schools by things such as class size, location, and community service requirement (*www.aamc.org/msar*). Every medical school has a different curriculum and style. This worksheet can help you determine which factors are important to you.

School name: _____

Factor	Ideal fit	Good fit	No opinion	Unsure	Not a fit	Notes
Course offerings						
Class size						
Location						
Research programs						
Technology						
Interviews and/or meetings with faculty						
Reputation						
Technology						
Tuition and financial aid						
Programs for minority or disadvantaged students						
Teaching methods						
Combined-degree offerings						
Campus tour						
Rural or community offerings						
Residency placement						

Impression of school: ❏ Favorable ❏ Undecided ❏ Unfavorable

Likelihood of applying: ❏ Will apply ❏ Undecided ❏ Unlikely to apply

Follow-up questions to ask: _____

Chapter 7

Applying to Medical School

Amanda Xi, MD
Resident, Henry Ford Hospital
Oakland University William Beaumont
(OUWB) School of Medicine
Class of 2015

Your journey to medical school may include moments when you feel overwhelmed, like when it's time to complete your medical school applications. In preparation for the application season, I met with my pre-health advisor for tips on how to stay organized. The AMCAS® [the American Medical College Application Service®] is used by almost every medical school in the country. To keep myself from feeling overwhelmed before starting my application, I read through the AMCAS Instruction Manual. From there, I requested transcripts, asked for letters of evaluation, and started a spreadsheet to keep track of schools, secondary applications, and notes from my interviews and communication with each school.

My recommendations for applicants are:
1. Work with your letter writers to set deadlines that allow them enough time to write high-quality letters, but also ensure that you comfortably meet your deadlines.
2. Prior to submitting anything—requests for letters, your personal statement, your AMCAS application—save a draft and reread it at a later time.

Take a deep breath and slowly exhale. Although the application process is arduous, with adequate preparation and organization, it will fly by!

Responsibilities of the Medical School Applicant

As a medical school applicant, you have certain responsibilities. These are reviewed at length at the end of this chapter, but some of the most critical are:

- Meeting all deadlines

- Completing the AMCAS application accurately

- Knowing the admission requirements at each school

- Promptly updating your AMCAS application with any change in contact information

- Responding promptly to interview invitations

- Filing for financial aid as soon as possible

- Withdrawing from the schools you will not attend

For more details, see "AAMC's Application and Acceptance Protocols for Applicants and Admission Officers" later in this chapter.

American Medical College Application Service®

You may have heard about the American Medical College Application Service (AMCAS®) from your pre-health advisor, career counselor, or even your classmates. AMCAS is a centralized medical school application processing service offered by the AAMC and used by almost every medical school in the country. (Schools that don't participate in AMCAS are listed on page 66.) This service does not screen applicants; rather, it provides admission officers with the information and tools they need to select the applicants who are the best fit for their institution.

AMCAS offers many benefits to applicants. The most obvious one is that it allows you to apply to as many medical schools as you want with a single application (although many schools require a secondary application, a topic discussed later in this chapter). It also provides applicants with a single point of transmission for official transcripts, letters of evaluation, and other supporting documentation.

Even if you're not yet ready to begin the application process, you can familiarize yourself with the process at *www.aamc.org/amcas*. There, you'll find information on the key steps involved in starting an application, an application overview, tips for completing the application, answers to frequently asked questions, and a comprehensive instruction manual.

If you have previously registered for the MCAT® exam, the Fee Assistance Program, or other AAMC services, you've already created an AAMC username and password and received an AAMC ID. Use this same information to access the AMCAS application site. If you don't already have an AAMC ID number, you'll need to register online to create a username and password before you begin your application.

AMCAS Application Sections

The AMCAS application is organized into nine sections. That might sound like a lot, but remember, you don't have to complete it all at once. You can save your work and return to your application as many times as you want until you finish and are ready to submit it. Here's an overview of what to expect:

1. **Identifying Information.** This section asks you to enter your name, birth information, and sex.

2. **Schools Attended.** Here, you will enter high school and college information. Once this section (and the identifying information section) is completed, you will be able to create a Transcript Request Form, which will help you request official transcripts from your registrar.

3. **Biographic Information.** You'll use this section to enter your contact information, citizenship status, legal residence, ethnicity, language(s) spoken, and other biographic information. Also, you'll indicate your immigration status in the Citizenship subsection. If your Deferred Action for Childhood Arrivals (DACA) application was approved by the U.S. government, select "DACA" from the designated drop-down list.

4. **Coursework.** You'll enter grades and credits for every course you've enrolled in at any U.S., U.S. territorial, or Canadian postsecondary institution that appears on your official college transcript(s). You're required to provide information for all the college-level courses you've taken, even if you took them during high school. For courses attempted through a study abroad program, carefully follow the instructions outlined in the AMCAS Instruction Manual. List study abroad coursework under the foreign college, the foreign listing of your home institution, or the organization at which it was attempted. Do not enter the coursework twice.

5. **Work/Activities.** Here, you'll enter any work and extracurricular activities, awards, honors, or publications that you'd like to bring to the attention of the medical schools. You may list up to 15 experiences. You'll then choose the three you consider to be the most meaningful and will be given1,325 characters to explain why each experience was particularly meaningful to you.

6. **Letters of Evaluation.** In this section, you'll provide information about people writing letters of evaluation on your behalf. You may want to review the AAMC's Letters of Evaluation Guidelines, a useful tool developed to help your letter writers. (This step is covered in more detail later in the chapter.)

7. **Medical Schools.** In this section, you'll designate the medical schools to which you want to submit an application. In addition, you can designate which letters of evaluation you wish to send to specific schools.

8. **Personal Statement.** Here, you'll compose an essay about why you want to go to medical school. (This is discussed more thoroughly later in this chapter.)

9. **Standardized Tests.** And finally … your MCAT® scores. In this section, you'll review your MCAT scores and enter any additional test information, such as GRE scores. Any MCAT scores from 2003 or later will automatically be released to AMCAS. Please note: It's important to include all the MCAT exams you're scheduled to take on your AMCAS application and update this information as appropriate after you submit your application.

Of course, this is just a simplified overview of the AMCAS application. Read the *AMCAS Instruction Manual* and explore the various resources for a more thorough understanding of the application on the AMCAS website at *www.aamc.org/amcas*.

Transcript Requests via AMCAS

In addition to completing your AMCAS application, you must request that official transcripts from all postsecondary institutions at which you've registered be sent to AMCAS. AMCAS provides a Transcript Request Form to facilitate this process with your registrar(s). If you've taken courses at a junior college, community college, trade school, or other professional school—regardless of whether credit was earned—within the United States, Canada, or U.S. territories, you must provide an official transcript from that institution. (This requirement also applies to any college courses you took in high school.) For most applicants, all official transcripts must be received no later than two weeks after the deadline date for application materials. Please refer to the *AMCAS Instruction Manual* at *www.aamc.org/amcasmanual* and the AMCAS website for detailed information about official transcript requirements.

Limited Changes After Submission

It's important to check your work carefully before you hit "submit" because you're limited in what changes you can make after submission. You can make changes to your contact information (such as addresses) and add schools or letters of evaluation, but other than that, your application will be submitted to schools exactly as it was completed.

Application Processing and Verification

Once AMCAS has received your submitted application and all required official transcripts from each postsecondary school where you were registered, the AMCAS verification process begins. AMCAS verifies the accuracy of your academic record by comparing the information you entered on your application with what's on your official transcripts. During the verification process, AMCAS converts transcript grades to AMCAS grades based on conversion information provided by colleges and universities and calculates an AMCAS GPA. The AMCAS GPA gives medical schools a standard way to compare each applicant's academic record. AMCAS GPAs may differ from the GPA shown on your records at the institutions you attended.

Once verification is complete, AMCAS makes your application and MCAT scores available to all the medical schools you designated (MCAT scores from 2003 and later are automatically included).

The Application and Admission Cycle

The AMCAS application usually opens to applicants in early May of each year and opens for submission in early June. Participating schools receive verified application data from AMCAS in late June.

The deadlines for receipt of primary applications to medical schools that participate in AMCAS are from the Early Decision Deadline in early August to mid-December (information on secondary applications is discussed later in this chapter). However, there's no single application timetable because each school establishes its own deadlines for receipt of required materials. You can find specific dates in medical schools' bulletins and websites and in the school listings on the Medical School Admission Requirements website (*www.aamc.org/msar*).

Medical schools vary in the timing of their admission decisions. Most schools use a system of "rolling admissions," selecting students for interviews and making admission decisions as applications are received, rather than waiting until after a specific deadline date to begin their evaluation process. All medical schools must wait until mid-October before they can start offering acceptance letters. You can find out if a medical school uses a rolling admissions system by checking its website.

For the 2015 AMCAS application cycle, students applied to 15.7 schools, on average. The U.S. medical schools that are not participating in AMCAS for the 2016 entering class are all in Texas. The seven public medical schools in Texas listed here participate in the Texas Medical and Dental School Application Service (TMDSAS) for those pursuing the MD degree. You can learn more about this application service and apply to these schools through TMDSAS at *www.utsystem.edu/tmdsas*. Applicants pursuing MD/PhD degrees at all but the Paul L. Foster School of Medicine *can* do so through AMCAS®, however.

- Texas A&M University System Health Science Center College of Medicine

- Texas Tech University Health Sciences Center School of Medicine

- Texas Tech University Health Sciences Center, El Paso, Paul L. Foster School of Medicine

- University of Texas Southwestern Medical Center at Dallas Southwestern Medical School

- University of Texas Medical School at Galveston

- University of Texas School of Medicine at Houston

- University of Texas School of Medicine at San Antonio

If you're interested in schools that do not participate in AMCAS, please contact them directly for application instructions.

You should also contact schools directly for application information if you wish to pursue a joint degree program, such as a BA/MD or an MD/PhD.

As far as interviews go, many admission committees begin meeting with candidates in the late summer and continue through spring. However, the majority of interviews are held during the winter months. (This part of the admission cycle is discussed in Chapter 8.) By March 30, medical schools will have issued enough acceptances to at least equal the size of their first-year entering class.

Personal Statements and Letters of Evaluation

As you'll learn in Chapter 8, "The Admission Decision," admission officers want to know more about you than just where you went to college, the courses you've taken, the grades you've earned, and how you scored on the MCAT exam. They want to know you on a more personal level. That's why an essay and letters of evaluation are integral components of your medical school application.

Your Personal Statement

Every applicant is required to submit a personal essay of up to 5,300 characters (about one page) in length. This is your opportunity to distinguish yourself from other applicants and provide admission officers with insights about why you're interested in medicine—and why you would be a dedicated and effective physician.

Most admission committees place significant weight on this section, so take the time to craft an organized, well-written, and compelling statement. Here are some questions you may want to consider while writing your essay:

- Why do you want a career in medicine?

- What motivates you to learn more about medicine?

- What should medical schools know about you that isn't described in other sections of the application?

In addition, you may wish to include information such as this:

- What special hardships, challenges, or obstacles have influenced your educational pursuits?

- Are you able to explain significant fluctuations in your academic record not explained elsewhere in your application?

It's a good idea to use specific examples in your essay. Instead of writing "Challenges in my childhood led me to consider medicine at an early age," write, "The summer I turned 8, my 11-year-old sister was diagnosed with neuroblastoma, and I witnessed firsthand the compassion and understanding with which the doctor dealt with my parents. It was during those first few difficult months that I decided I wanted to be a physician."

Additionally, ensure that your essay is interesting, follows a logical and orderly flow, and relates to your reasons for choosing medicine and/or why you believe you'll be successful in medical school and as a physician. Beyond that, be sure to use correct grammar and avoid typographical errors and misspellings.

For MD/PhD Applicants

If you're applying to MD/PhD programs, you'll be required to write two additional essays: a relatively brief one focusing on your reasons for pursuing the combined degree and a lengthier one (about three pages) describing your research activities. You can read more about these additional essays in the *AMCAS Instruction Manual* or get further guidance from your pre-health advisor or career counselor.

Early Decision Programs

One of your first decisions will be whether to apply to a medical school through the Early Decision Program (EDP) or the regular application process. Although criteria for accepting EDP applicants vary among schools, programs frequently require that applicants show extraordinary credentials. A small percentage of applicants apply through the EDP, and only about half of medical schools offer the option. You can learn more about program requirements at *www.aamc.org/students/applying/*.

Letters of Evaluation

In the Letters of Evaluation section, you'll provide information about the people writing your letters. Although you can add up to 10 letter entries, medical schools do not necessarily wish to receive 10 letters per applicant. Most schools request only two or three letters. (You can find the minimum and maximum letters accepted by each school on the Medical School Admission Requirements website.) AMCAS accepts letters of evaluation on behalf of participating medical schools. This service enables medical schools to receive all letters electronically from AMCAS and allows letter writers to send their letter to AMCAS, rather than to each individual school. AMCAS permits additional letters so that you have the option to designate specific letters for specific schools. For more information and a current list of schools participating in the AMCAS Letter Service, see *www.aamc.org/aboutamcasletters*.

Medical schools have various requirements for letters of evaluation, but they all require letters in one form or another. If your college has a pre-health advisor, medical schools will probably require a letter from him or her (or from the pre-health committee, if your school has one), as well as a letter from at least one faculty member. In instances where there is no pre-health advisor, many medical schools may ask for additional letters from faculty and often specify that at least one comes from a science professor.

Some medical schools don't specify who should write your letters and welcome additional letters beyond the required ones. However, be aware of any limits on the number they will accept. In all cases, you should review medical schools' websites or the Medical School Admission Requirements website for information on specific letter requirements (*www.aamc.org/msar*).

Medical schools want letters from people who are in a position to judge your ability to be successful in medical school, which includes not only your academic capabilities and accomplishments, but also your personal characteristics and skills.

Secondary Applications

Your primary application is your AMCAS application, and it provides admission officers with much of the information they need. However, most medical schools also require a school-specific, or "secondary," application because it allows them to assess students' reasons for applying to that particular school. (Medical schools will notify you if they would like you to fill out a secondary application, although you can also find out by looking at their profiles on the Medical School Admission Requirements website.) Secondary applications may call for additional letters of evaluation, supplemental writing samples, and updated transcripts. Go to the websites of the medical schools you're interested in to learn more.

Application Fees

Medical school application fees fall into four general categories:

• *AMCAS Application.* For the 2016 application cycle, the AMCAS application fee plus designation to one school was $160, and it cost $37 for each additional school. Check the AMCAS website for the latest application fee information. Remember, some schools don't use AMCAS, and you may pay different fees in those instances.

• *Secondary Application.* In 2015, fees for secondary applications ranged from $0 to $200.

• *College Service Fees.* Your college registrar may charge a small fee to send your transcript to AMCAS. Occasionally, you'll incur a fee to send your letters of evaluation to AMCAS.

• *MCAT Exam Fees.* Although technically not part of the application fee, the costs associated with the MCAT exam are a necessary component of the overall process. The initial registration fee for the MCAT exam is currently $305 and covers the cost of the exam and distribution of your scores. In addition, you may incur fees for late registration, changes to your registration, or testing at international test sites. You can read more about the MCAT exam in Chapter 5 and get up-to-date information on the MCAT website (*www.aamc.org/mcat*).

For more information on application fees, go to *www.aamc.org/first/factsheets*.

Criminal Background Check

The AAMC facilitates a national background check on all accepted applicants to participating medical schools via Certiphi Screening, Inc. (a Vertical Screen® Company). This service provides required background checks to medical schools and prevents you from paying additional fees to each medical school to run these checks independently. For more information, go to *www.aamc.org/amcascbc*.

Be aware that participating medical schools may also require applicants to undergo a separate national background check process, if it's required by their own institutional regulations or by applicable state law.

Fee Assistance Program

The AAMC believes that the cost of applying to medical school should not be a financial barrier to people interested in becoming physicians.

The AAMC Fee Assistance Program helps MCAT examinees and AMCAS applicants who, without financial assistance, would be unable to take the MCAT exam and apply to medical schools that use the AMCAS application. Visit the Fee Assistance Program website for details about the program's eligibility requirements and to access the application.

You'll be able to use your Fee Assistance Program award benefits for up to two calendar years. Benefits expire on December 31 the year after they are awarded, regardless of when in the year you apply for, and receive, the award. **You may only apply for fee assistance once per calendar year. Fee Assistance Program benefits are never retroactive**.

Applicants who are approved for fee assistance in 2016 will receive MCAT and Medical School Admission Requirements benefits.

MCAT Benefits

- Reduced registration fees for up to four MCAT exam dates until December 31, 2017
- Reduced rescheduling fees for MCAT exam dates until December 31, 2017
- A suite of MCAT prep products and resources (you'll receive more details about these benefits if you're awarded fee assistance)
- Up to $500 toward an updated psychoeducational or medical evaluation if it's required to support your MCAT accommodations application

Regardless of how many times you're awarded fee assistance, you'll receive MCAT prep product benefits only once.

Medical School Admission Requirements Benefits

- Complimentary access to the Medical School Admission Requirements website until December 31, 2017 ($54 value)
- AMCAS Benefits
- Waiver for all AMCAS fees for one application submission with up to 15 medical school designations ($664 value)

Additional fees will be charged for each medical school designation beyond the initial set of 15.

Special Note About Deferred Entry

In recent years, most medical schools have developed delayed matriculation policies to allow accepted applicants to defer entry without giving up their spot. Deferrals are granted only after acceptance. These programs usually require that you submit a written request, and some schools also ask for a report at the end of the deferral period. Matriculation delays are usually granted for one year, although some schools occasionally defer for longer periods of time. Some institutions may require delayed matriculants to sign an agreement not to apply to other medical schools in the interim, while others permit applications to other schools. If you're interested in this option, you should seek specific information from schools you applied to. You can find out more about each school's policy by viewing their profile in the Medical School Admission Requirements website.

Gap Year and Career Changers

If you're applying to medical school after spending more than a year out of college, you'll need to get transcripts from any additional coursework or degree programs you've completed since your undergraduate graduation. Even if you applied previously to medical school, you'll need to resubmit official transcripts. Also, you must resubmit letters of evaluation to AMCAS each time you apply.

For more information about gap years, please look for the "Making the Most of Your Gap Year" fact sheet on the Aspiring Docs website, *students-residents.aamc.org/applying-medical-school/article/making-most-your-gap-year*.

AAMC's Application and Acceptance Protocols for Applicants and Admission Officers

The AAMC recommends the following to help ensure that all MD and MD/PhD applicants receive timely notification about the outcome of their application and protect schools and programs from having unfilled positions in their entering classes. These protocols are often referred to as "traffic rules" by admission officers and pre-health advisors. Prospective applicants, their advisors, and admission staff at medical schools and programs should all be aware of these application and acceptance protocols for applicants.

What This Means for You (the Applicant)

These protocols were developed to ensure fairness for both applicants and medical schools. By reading and acknowledging the guidelines, as well as agreeing to adhere to them, applicants and medical schools affirm that they understand the timelines and stresses involved with making these important decisions. They also acknowledge that their decisions affect the choices of other applicants and schools that are also in the midst of making acceptance and admission decisions. Admission officers know that most applicants are anxiously awaiting notifications, but their committees are also diligently working to build the next class for their medical schools. These rules help ensure that everyone does their best to make timely, ethical, and fair decisions during this hectic time. The protocols are periodically reviewed by the AAMC's Committee on Admission and approved by the AAMC's Council of Deans. The protocols that follow were approved by the AAMC Council of Deans Administrative Board in September 2014.

Protocols for Applicants

The AAMC recommends that as an applicant to an MD or MD/PhD program, you:

1. Understand and comply with these applicant responsibilities as well as with the application, acceptance, and admissions procedures at each school or program to which you apply.

2. Provide accurate and truthful information in all aspects of your application, interview(s), acceptance, and admissions processes for each school or program to which you apply.

3. Submit all application documents (e.g., primary and secondary application forms, transcript(s), letters of evaluation/recommendation, fees, etc.) on or before the school or program's published deadline.

4. Notify all relevant medical school application services of any change, permanent or temporary, to your contact information (e.g., mailing address, telephone number, and email address).

5. If you will be unavailable for an extended period of time (e.g., during foreign travel, vacation, or holidays) during the application/admission process:

    a. Provide instructions regarding your application and the authority to respond to any offers of acceptance to a parent or other responsible individual in your absence.
    b. Inform all schools or programs at which your application remains under consideration of this person's name and contact information.

6. Respond promptly to a school's or program's invitation for an interview. If you cannot appear for a scheduled interview, notify the school or program immediately that you need to cancel via the school or program's preferred communication method.

7. Begin the steps necessary to determine your eligibility for financial aid. This may include filling out need-analysis forms early and having your parents (when required) complete the appropriate income tax forms.

8. In fairness to other applicants, if you have decided before April 30 not to attend a medical school or program that has offered you an acceptance, promptly withdraw your application from the school(s) or program(s) by written correspondence or their preferred communication method.

9. If you receive an offer of acceptance from more than one school or program, choose the school that you will enroll in by April 30. Then, promptly withdraw your application, by written correspondence, from all other schools or programs that have offered you an acceptance.

10. Withdraw your application from consideration at all other schools or programs as soon as you enroll, or start an orientation program prior to enrollment, at a U.S. or Canadian school or program.

Note: If any date falls on a weekend and/or holiday, the recommendation(s) will apply to the following business day.

Protocols for Admission Officers

The AAMC recommends that each MD- or MD/PhD-granting school or program:

1. Comply with established procedures to:
   a. Annually publish, amend, and adhere to its application, acceptance, and admission procedures.
   b. Abide by all conditions of participation agreements with application services (if using).

2. Promptly communicate admissions decisions:
   a. By October 1, notify Early Decision applicants and the American Medical College Application Service® (AMCAS®) of Early Decision Program (EDP) admission actions.
   b. From October 15 to March 15, notify AMCAS within five business days of all admission actions, either written or verbal, that have been communicated to an applicant.
   c. From March 16 to the first day of class, notify AMCAS within two business days of all admissions acceptance, withdrawal, or deferral actions, either written or verbal, that have been communicated to an applicant. All admission actions are listed and defined on the AAMC website.
   d. An acceptance offer is defined as the point at which a medical school communicates a written or verbal acceptance offer to an applicant.
   e. An acceptance offer to any dual-degree program that occurs after an initial acceptance should follow the above timelines.

3. Notify all regular MD program applicants of their acceptance on or after October 15 of each admission cycle, but no earlier. Schools and programs may notify applicants of admissions decisions other than acceptance prior to October 15.

4. By March 15 of the matriculation year, issue a number of acceptance offers at least equal to the expected number of students in its first-year entering class and report those acceptance actions to AMCAS.

5. On or before April 30, permit ALL applicants (except for EDP applicants):
   a. A minimum of two weeks to respond to their acceptance offer.
   b. To hold acceptance offers or a waitlist position from any other schools or programs without penalty (i.e., scholarships).

6. After April 30, implement school-specific procedures for accepted applicants who, without adequate explanation, continue to hold one or more places at other schools or programs.
   a. Each school or program should permit applicants:
      1. A minimum of five business days to respond to an acceptance offer. This may be reduced to a minimum of two business days within 30 days of the start of orientation.
      2. Submit a statement of intent, a deposit, or both.
   b. Recognize the challenges of applicants with multiple acceptance offers, applicants who have not yet received an acceptance offer, and applicants who have not yet been informed about financial aid opportunities at schools to which they have been accepted.
   c. Permit applicants who have been accepted or who have been granted a deferral to remain on other schools' or programs' wait lists. Also, permit these applicants to withdraw if they later receive an acceptance offer from a preferred school or program.

7. Each school's pre-enrollment deposit should not exceed $100 and (except for EDP applicants) be refundable until April 30. If the applicant enrolls at the school, the school should credit the deposit toward tuition. Schools should not require additional deposits or matriculation fees prior to matriculation.

8. On or after May 15, any school that plans to make an acceptance offer to an applicant who has already been accepted to, or granted a deferral by, another school or program, must ensure that the other school or program is advised of this offer at the time it is issued (written or verbally) to the applicant. This notification should be made immediately by telephone and email by the close of business on the same day. The communication should contain the applicant's name and AAMC ID number, the program being offered (e.g., MD only, joint program), and the date through which the offer is valid. Schools and programs should communicate fully with each other with respect to anticipated late roster changes in order to minimize inter-school miscommunication and misunderstanding, as well as to prevent unintended vacant positions in a school's first-year entering class.

9. No school or program should make an acceptance offer, either verbal or written, to any individual who has officially matriculated/enrolled in or begun an orientation program immediately prior to enrollment at an LCME-accredited medical school. Medical programs should enter a matriculation action for students in AMCAS immediately upon the start of enrollment or the orientation immediately preceding enrollment.

10. Each school should treat all letters of evaluation submitted in support of an application as confidential, except in those states with applicable laws to the contrary. The contents of a letter of evaluation should not be revealed to an applicant at any time.

Note: If any date falls on a weekend and/or holiday, the recommendation(s) will apply to the following business day.

AMCAS Reports Provided to Medical Schools

To help medical schools adhere to the application and acceptance protocols, AMCAS provides the following reports to schools.

- School Acceptance Report

  Schools begin receiving this report on September 1, and it includes a list of all accepted applicants at that school. On February 10, this report also begins to include "multiple acceptance data." This means that if a medical school accepts you, they will be able to see a list of any other schools that have also accepted you. Schools can never see how many schools you applied to or if you received a rejection from other schools.

- National Acceptance Report

  This report is released beginning on April 1 and includes a list of all AMCAS applicants who have been granted at least one acceptance. If an applicant has more than one acceptance, all schools are listed. After October 31, this report also includes the applicant's school of matriculation.

- Joint Acceptance Report

  This report is also available beginning on April 1. It only includes applicants who are accepted by more than one school. A school viewing this report will see a list of their accepted applicants who are also holding acceptances at one or more other schools. This report also includes applicants with admission actions of deferral, withdrawn after acceptance, and rescinded acceptance.

It's important to keep in mind that:

- Schools can never see how many schools you applied to

- If you're accepted, schools can see other schools that also accepted you starting on February 10 of the application year

- After April 30 of the application year, schools can follow their own policies on how to handle applicants who continue to hold more than one acceptance

Worksheets at the end of chapters in this guide are available in fillable PDF format at www.aamc.org/msar-resources.

Be sure that you're familiar with your school's policy on letters of evaluation. It may provide a committee or composite letter on your behalf. If you are responsible for selecting individuals to write your letters of evaluation, you should look for someone who knows you well and can speak to your readiness for medical school. These letters can be very valuable, so you should be thoughtful in selecting who you ask to write on your behalf.

How to choose an appropriate letter writer and keep track of your interactions with them

Maintain a journal or log that indicates where you've worked and volunteered and what classes you've taken. It's important to keep track of the faculty members and supervisors you work with because those people will likely be able to write you a strong letter of evaluation when it comes time to apply. Keep notes about time spent working on particular projects so you can remember what you did. When you finish working with a particular person, you can go ahead and ask them to write you a reference letter.

Letter writer's name	Why this person would be a good advocate for me	Contact info	Letter complete?
_____	_____	_____	❏ Yes!
	_____	_____	
	_____	_____	
_____	_____	_____	❏ Yes!
	_____	_____	
	_____	_____	
_____	_____	_____	❏ Yes!
	_____	_____	
	_____	_____	
_____	_____	_____	❏ Yes!
	_____	_____	
	_____	_____	

Chapter 8

The Admission Decision

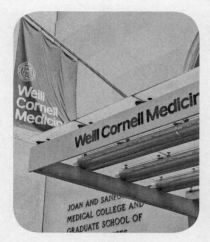

The Meyer Building for Research and Education at Weill Cornell Medicine.

While expectations vary from school to school, most look for students who can handle challenging coursework and demonstrate sound judgment, compassion, and selflessness. In my experience, admission committees also look for students with exceptional personal initiative in the form of leadership, creativity, research, or service.

Excelling in rigorous upper-level courses and doing well on the MCAT® exam show that you can handle medical school coursework. Demonstrating good judgment, compassion, and leadership through experience, letters of evaluation, and a personal statement shows that you exhibit the personal qualities of a good physician.

Before submitting your application, ask a pre-health advisor or mentor to read it because no matter how closely you've checked it, a fresh pair of eyes may find something you missed. Ask trusted friends or family members to give you feedback, too. Ask, 'How would you describe me based on what you read? Did my essay hold your attention? Was anything confusing? Did you notice any typos?'

Ultimately, the committee screeners attempt to identify the applicants most likely to succeed academically, build a dynamic and diverse learning environment, care for patients diligently, and become leaders in medicine.

– Lori Nicolaysen
Assistant Dean of Admissions
Weill Cornell Medical College

The Holistic Review of Medical School Applicants

What does holistic mean, and how does it affect the admission review process?

Holistic review is a flexible, individualized way of assessing an applicant. The review considers a balance of an applicant's experiences, attributes, and academic metrics (E-A-M) and, when taken together, how the individual may contribute value as a medical student and future physician. When admission committees select individual applicants, they intentionally try to create a broadly diverse class to help fulfill their school's mission.

Each medical school's admission office evaluates applicants based on the mission, goals, and diversity interests of that institution. Admission committees must decide which applicants will best serve the needs of their patients and community and the medical profession at large. They seek a broadly diverse student body because diversity has consistently been shown to drive educational and professional excellence. Schools look for applicants who have developed a track record that demonstrates the knowledge, skills, attitudes, and behaviors that will best prepare them to navigate challenges and thrive as both learners and physicians. Depending on its mission, one school might look for applicants who demonstrate service to communities underserved by the current health care system, while another may seek applicants who have shown creativity and independent productivity in scholarly activities.

Admission officers carefully review a multitude of criteria—rather than focusing on just one or two facets—to gain an appreciation of the "whole" person. Many applicants erroneously believe that admission officers weigh high GPAs and MCAT® scores above all else. While these academic metrics are important components of the admission decision, they are only one part of the overall package. An applicant's ability to balance multiple priorities and responsibilities as well as the resilience they've shown in handling various issues is considered along with grades and MCAT scores. This helps explain why there are many cases in which a high-scoring student with a near-perfect GPA may not get into medical school, and why others with scores and grades below the average do.

Admission decisions involve more than academic metrics.

Experiences

Your experiences convey a lot about your interests, responsibilities, capabilities, and knowledge. As a result, medical schools take a close look at what you've learned from where you've been up to this stage in your life. It helps them gauge not only how likely you are to be successful in their programs, but also to what degree you'll support their mission and contribute as a physician.

The chapter on undergraduate preparation mentioned how important your extracurricular activities may be to an admission committee—and not just those clubs and organizations within your college, but also outside of school. Your experiences—particularly those related to medicine or research—are an important component that affects your competitiveness as a candidate. For instance, if you are balancing a 20-to-30-hour-a-week job to pay for school while attending classes or have responsibilities caring for a younger sibling or elderly relative, those experiences are important to share with admission committees. They communicate information about your different attributes and provide additional context for interpreting your grades. Your experiences—and the insights you gained from them—also help admission committees identify what's unique about you and how you may contribute to their school and the practice of medicine.

Beyond that, the degree to which you contributed to and participated in these activities is vital. Medical schools value a demonstration of true commitment, so if you've made a significant contribution to or impact on an organization or taken on increasing levels of responsibility, you'll want to make that clear to the admission committee. They're interested not only in what you've done, but how you think those experiences have influenced who you are and what you want to do. A series of short-term involvements (volunteering a day here, spending an afternoon there, and so forth) does not really convey a deep interest in the area, and this underlying motivation is transparent to admission officials. They're looking for substantial, committed participation in areas that are truly important to you. Only then are they able to gain some insights into your real interests and judge how well your goals and their missions align.

Again, the mission of each school will play a large part in how your experience is evaluated. For example, institutions whose goal is to increase the number of physicians practicing in underserved areas will focus attention on the summer you spent volunteering in a free clinic or doing rural or urban community outreach on health promotion. In general, medical schools especially value community and volunteer experience related to the health care field.

Concept of "Distance Traveled"

Here's another thing to consider: Admission officers are likely to place significance on any obstacles or hardships you've overcome to get to this point in your education. This concept, known as "distance traveled," refers to those life challenges you've faced and conquered. Medical schools view these instances as admirable experiences indicative of some very positive traits, such as resilience and persistence. As with other experiences, you can help the admission committee better understand and appreciate your unique contributions by not only describing the experiences, but also describing how they have helped influence you and your desire to be a physician.

Experiences likely to be important to admission committees:

- Serving as the primary caregiver for an ill family member

- Overcoming obstacles or hardships

- Being employed (especially if medically related)

- Participating in research

- Working, volunteering, or shadowing in a health care setting

- Participating in and leading community-based or volunteer organizations

Attributes

Admission committees want to know if you have what it takes to become a competent and compassionate doctor. This includes the ability to master the science and medicine behind it all, of course, but it also requires that you have some key personal attributes. They use various methods to determine whether you have those attributes. While personal experiences such as volunteering for three consecutive summers at a medical clinic certainly convey dedication and help demonstrate your proficiency in these areas, admission committees will look to your personal statement, letters of evaluation, and interviews to gauge whether you have the desire to build on these experiences in medical school.

Are you empathetic? Do you have integrity? Can you communicate effectively and with people different from yourself? Traits such as these are necessary to develop into the kind of physician needed for the future.

Examples of attributes likely to be important to admission committees:

- Adaptability
- Critical thinking
- Integrity
- Logical reasoning
- Oral communication skills
- Personal maturity
- Reliability
- Self-discipline

- Work habits
- Compassion
- Cultural competence
- Intellectual curiosity
- Motivation for medicine
- Persistence
- Professionalism
- Resilience

Medical schools analyze a broad range of attributes, including those related to the applicant's skills and abilities, personal and professional characteristics, and demographic factors.

- **Skills and abilities** could include active listening, critical thinking, and multilingual ability.

- **Personal and professional characteristics** could include resilience, intellectual curiosity, and empathy.

- **Demographic factors** could include socioeconomic status, race, and gender.

In addition to these general qualities, medical schools give weight to specific characteristics that align with their missions. Examples could include research inquisitiveness, empathy, teamwork, curiosity, and a desire for knowledge about health care delivery systems.

Academic Metrics

Admission committees need to determine whether you have the academic skills and knowledge necessary to succeed in medical school. Committee members will consider your academic record and MCAT scores to measure your knowledge and abilities objectively.

Academic History

Your academic history helps admission committees determine whether your study skills, persistence, course of study, and grades predict success at their medical school. Committee members carefully review your college transcript and consider:

- Grades earned in each course and laboratory

- Grade trends in the last two years of schooling

- Number of credit hours carried in each academic period

- Distribution of coursework among the biological, physical, and social sciences and the humanities

- Need for remediation of unsatisfactory academic work

- Number of incomplete grades and course withdrawals

- Number of years taken to complete the degree program

- The amount of advanced coursework completed in addition to the standard prerequisites and requirements

MCAT Scores

Admission committees can better predict success when they add MCAT scores into the mix. That's because there can be significant differences in grading scales and standards from college to college, and MCAT scores provide a standardized measure by which to compare applicants. In fact, the ability of admission officers to predict who will be successful in the first two years of their programs increases by as much as 50 percent (gauging by first- and second-year medical school grades) when they look at MCAT scores in conjunction with undergraduate GPAs as opposed to grades alone.

As a result, the better your grades and the higher your scores, the more likely you are to be accepted. It is important to remember that there's still a wide range of MCAT scores and GPAs found among accepted applicants and that those are used in conjunction with other factors, as discussed earlier in this chapter.

Making the Evaluation

Admission committees gauge all three of these areas—experiences, attributes, and academic metrics—and how they relate to each other in several ways. Although each medical school establishes its own criteria, schools usually prefer applicants who balanced science and humanities coursework, carried respectable course loads, and, generally speaking, earned 3.0–4.0 GPAs (on a 4.0 scale).

Several elements within the application process speak to your experiences and attributes. Your personal statement, as mentioned in Chapter 7, gives you the opportunity to tell committee members about your extracurricular activities, distance traveled, volunteer efforts, and medical-related work experience. The personal attributes that accompany these activities can often be inferred. For example, a role as an officer in a school club conveys leadership experience. Working in a medical clinic summer after summer demonstrates motivation for medicine. A long history of volunteering with fundraisers for cancer research suggests teamwork and compassion. Applicants can speak to these experiences in their statements and during interviews to further underscore these connections.

Your letters of evaluation, also described in Chapter 7, attest to your personal attributes. Ask your professors and advisor (and other evaluators) to address your persistence, strong work habits, and self-discipline. (The faculty and administrative staff at your undergraduate school will know how to craft a letter, but for others, you might want to suggest a few key concepts.)

Then there are the academic metrics. As you may know, your academic record is part of your AMCAS application and includes both your college transcript(s) and MCAT scores. From there, committee members can determine whether you have the grades, range of coursework, and foundation of knowledge they seek in their successful applicants.

Schools consider your experiences, attributes, and academic metrics in combination. Together, they give shape to what you, as an applicant, may contribute to their medical school and to health care at large. So keep this in mind: It's not only about what you did and what you know, but it's also about who you are and what you bring to the learning environment and the medical profession.

The Interview Is Key

If you've been invited to an interview, you should feel confident because you've already impressed your reviewers with your strong personal statement, background, letters of evaluation, and academic history. The interview day gives you a chance to tour the medical school's facility and meet the students, faculty, and staff you may be interacting with for the next several years. Take this opportunity to assess the culture and learning environment and explore whether the school might be a good fit for you. Now, you have an opportunity to "shine." Medical schools usually interview three, four, even five times as many applicants as their class size, and this is why the interview is likely to be the number one determining factor at this phase in the assessment. Other factors include how you interact with others and how you react to stressful questions.

The fact that interviews are given at all is a significant distinction of medical schools because some professional schools don't require them. The medical school interview attests to the degree to which admission officers seek—and medical schools value—qualities and characteristics such as empathy, self-awareness, communication ability, and interpersonal skills that can best be judged in a direct interview situation. You can take these steps to ensure you're prepared for it.

Know the Basics

Whether it's for a new job or for a seat in a medical school's entering class, certain similarities exist in all interviewing situations. A good start is to review any interviewing books in your school's library or pre-health advisor's office, find out whether your advisor or pre-med club offers a mock-interview session, and search online for tips and interview resources. The Aspiring Docs library offers two fact sheets that describe the most common types of interviews and tips on how to prepare yourself. Check out the fact sheets at *www.aamc.org/aspiringdocs*.

Know What Type of Interview to Expect

It helps to be ready for several different interview formats. At some schools, interviews are held with individual admission committee members; at others, group interviews are the norm. While most interviews are held on the medical school campus, some schools have designated interviewers in different geographic regions to minimize time and expense for applicants. (Information about a school's interview policies and procedures is usually provided to applicants in the initial stages of the selection process.) Check the Medical School Admission Requirements website to find the type of interviews offered, such as one-on-one, panel, or video interviews (*www.aamc.org/msar*).

Be Comfortable with Different Interviewing Styles

You probably have had some experience interviewing for summer and part-time jobs (and possibly for your undergraduate school), so it won't surprise you that interviewers have their own styles and follow different formats. Some interviewers follow a structured design, asking questions from a predetermined list and assigning numeric scores to each answer. Others prefer a more free-flowing arrangement and provide the applicant with a greater degree of open input. Still others fall somewhere in the middle.

Do Your Research

Being able to speak knowledgeably about the medical school shows that you're interested and invested in this particular program. Investigate the school thoroughly by reviewing its profile on the Medical School Admission Requirements website (*www.aamc.org/msar*), the school's website, the information packet sent to you, and any articles you can find. Your time is limited, so don't waste it by asking questions already answered on their website, in their materials, or on the Medical School Admission Requirements website. Try to talk with current students to get an accurate sense of what the school is like from a student perspective. You'll want to impress your interviewer not only with your potential for success, but also with your interest in the specific institution. You can demonstrate these qualities through your answers to the interviewer's questions, as well as by the questions you ask.

Be Ready to Ask Questions

There will come a point in your interview when you'll be asked if you have any questions, and it's an opportunity you don't want to pass up. Not only can you clarify any remaining issues, but you'll have another way to demonstrate your commitment, astuteness, and interest in that particular school. With that in mind, you'll want to prepare two or three questions specific to that school. Need a way to generate ideas? Check out the AAMC's "Thirty-Five Questions I Wish I Had Asked" at *www.aamc.org/35questions*.

Practice

Most admission committee members are experienced interviewers who want to learn about the "real" person you are. Be honest and open during your meeting and do not try to just give the answers you think the interviewer wants to hear. Try to keep the interview conversational. If you're apprehensive about the process, asking a trusted advisor or friend to conduct mock interviews with you can help build your confidence.

Remember, the interview is an opportunity to discuss your personal history and motivation for pursuing a career in medicine. It also gives you a chance to address any aspects of your application that merit emphasis or explanation. Be sure to present yourself in the best possible light by preparing thoroughly for your meeting. Think about how you conduct yourself among current students and staff during informal meetings, too. Every interaction can create an impression of who you are, and how you present yourself usually comes up during a post-interview discussion.

A Few Last Reminders for Your Interview Day

When it comes to what to wear, a good rule of thumb is to dress for the job you seek. In short, look professional. Your interview is likely to be coupled with a tour of the campus, so be sure to wear shoes and an outfit that you're comfortable walking in.

Your interview day is a long one. You'll be doing a lot of talking and meeting numerous people. It's okay to bring a water bottle or drink with you. It's very important to be aware that everyone on campus you encounter is someone who can give feedback about you—positive and negative. Be sure to use good manners, be courteous to all, and show your enthusiasm. Lastly, keep your phone out of sight and on silent. You should not have it out at any time during the interview or campus tour. Remember, the people you speak with are not only evaluating your academic potential, but they're also seeing how you conduct yourself professionally and whether you're a good fit for their medical school.

Your Interview Rights and Responsibilities

Although interviewers are instructed by admission officers and guided by federal statutes on what are unfair or discriminatory preadmission inquiries, there may be an occasion when an interviewer asks an inappropriate question. (See examples in box at right.)

You have the right not to answer what you sense is an inappropriate question. If such a question is asked, try to relax and provide a thoughtful and articulate response (two essential characteristics of a good physician). You may also respectfully decline to answer the question and explain that you were advised not to answer questions that you sensed were inappropriate.

You have the responsibility to report being asked an inappropriate question to help prevent further occurrences. Medical schools have the responsibility to establish procedures that enable applicants to report such incidents in a confidential manner. Medical schools should inform you of these procedures prior to interviews and assure you that reporting an incident will not bias your evaluation.

If a medical school did not inform you of its procedures and an incident occurs, use these guidelines. If possible, report in confidence to an admission officer during the interview day the interviewer's name and the interview question(s) asked. Otherwise, email this information to an admission officer within 24 hours of the interview, noting the date and time of the incident. Furthermore, you have the right to ask if another interview is deemed necessary to ensure an unbiased evaluation of your application to that medical school.

Some interviewers use the interview to assess how well you function under stress and may purposely ask challenging questions to observe how you respond under pressure. How you communicate will be a critical part of the encounter; however, this does not give an interviewer the right to ask you inappropriate questions in their attempt to challenge you during the interview.

Examples of inappropriate questions:

Q. *What is your race, ethnicity, religion, sexual orientation, political affiliation, marital status, opinion on abortion and/or euthanasia, income, value of your home, credit score, etc.?*

Q. *Are you planning on having children during medical school?*

Q. *Do you have any disabilities?*

Q. *Will you require special accommodations?*

Q. *Have you ever been arrested?*

Q. *Have you ever done drugs?*

Q. *How old are you?*

Sample responses to inappropriate questions:

Q. *What are your plans for expanding your family during medical school?*

A. Can you please clarify your question? I want to make sure that I'm providing information that is most relevant to my candidacy.

Q. *Have you ever done drugs?*

A. I am uncomfortable discussing my medical history and possible use of prescription medication.

 Worksheets at the end of chapters in this guide are available in fillable PDF format at www.aamc.org/msar-resources.

As you research the medical schools you're interested in attending, use this worksheet to keep track of questions you think you may want to ask during your interview. Print or save this page for individual schools, and review it the night before your interview or bring it with you. You can find many questions here: *www.aamc.org/35questions*.

Name of Medical School: _____

Type of Interview: _____

Date of Interview: _____

Questions about:

1. Curriculum _____
   _____
   _____

2. Student Involvement _____
   _____
   _____

3. Special Programs _____
   _____
   _____

4. Financial Aid _____
   _____
   _____

5. Facilities _____
   _____
   _____

6. Academic Evaluations _____
   _____
   _____

7. Student Support _____
   _____
   _____

8. Residency Placements _____
   _____
   _____

9. Other _____
   _____

Chapter 9

Applicant and Acceptee Data

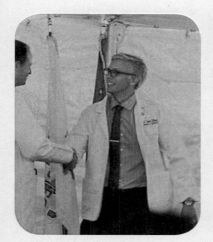

"When applying to medical school, it's difficult not to transform yourself into a number—well, two numbers: your MCAT® score and GPA. While these figures impact your application success, they are only two facets.

I often found myself riddled with self-doubt during that difficult 'glide year.' Was my MCAT score high enough? Would admissions committees overlook that low grade? I had to remember that I was more than a mathematical index on a percentile chart. I was an enthusiastic applicant and a lover of people, and I had plenty of clinical experiences and medical exposure to prove it.

Luke P. Burns
MD Candidate
University of California, San Diego
School of Medicine
Class of 2018

Applying to medical school is a constant assault on your self-esteem as you strive to meet the high standards you set for yourself. Be realistic, but don't be ruthless. Know your weaknesses, but celebrate your strengths. The skills you develop before medical school will inform you for the rest of your life. And those numbers that got you into medical school? They never matter again."

This chapter summarizes data about the entire applicant pool, as well as about accepted applicants and people who weren't accepted for the 2015 entering class. The data, from the AAMC Applicant Matriculant File, are accurate as of October 15, 2015. In the figures:

- "All applicants" refers to all applicants to the 2015 entering class

- "Accepted applicants" refers to those accepted to at least one medical school

- "Not-accepted applicants" refers to those not accepted to any medical school

We include data related to performance on the MCAT exam, undergraduate GPA and major, gender, age, medical/clinical and other experiences, and race and ethnicity.

A Quick Look at the 2015 Entering Class

- In 2014–2015, 52,550 people applied to the 2015 entering class at all MD-granting medical schools in the United States.

- By the fall of 2015, 21,647 applicants had been offered an acceptance to at least one medical school, and 20,631 accepted applicants had matriculated.

The accepted applicants had broad ranges of MCAT® scores and undergraduate grade point averages (GPAs) and a wide variety of personal characteristics and life experiences. Both male and female applicants were distributed across numerous racial and ethnic groups. Although a few applied through the Early Decision Program, the vast majority used the regular application process. A small number of accepted applicants—about 1,000—chose not to matriculate in 2015.

Performance on the MCAT Exam

Figure 9.1 summarizes the overall performance of 2015 applicants on the MCAT exam. It shows that the 2015 applicants achieved total scores from 4 to 45; the largest number achieved a total score of 31. Accepted applicants had total scores ranging from 14 to 45; about 15 accepted applicants had a total score of 17 or below (an average of almost 6 on each section of the test). The number of accepted applicants exceeded the number of not-accepted applicants starting at a total score of 31. (Please note that these scores reflect the scale of the MCAT exam administered before 2015. The current MCAT exam has a different score scale. For more information, see Chapter 5.)

No score on a single MCAT section and no total MCAT score will "guarantee" admission to medical school. Figure 9.1 shows that a substantial number of applicants with total MCAT scores of 30 and above were not accepted. This finding reveals the importance of factors other than MCAT performance—including undergraduate academic performance and a variety of personal characteristics and experiences—in the medical student selection process.

Figure 9.1. MCAT total numeric score distribution, 2015 applicants.

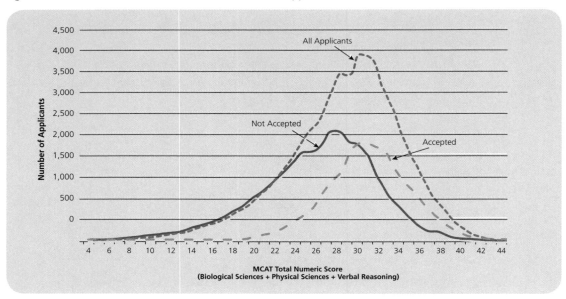

Source: AAMC Data Warehouse.

Undergraduate Grade Point Average

Figure 9.2 presents information about the undergraduate academic performance of 2015 applicants. All applicants had cumulative total undergraduate GPAs from just under 2.0 to 4.0, and most were between 3.75 and 4.0. Accepted applicants' total undergraduate GPAs ranged from just under 2.0 to 4.0, and about

100 had total undergraduate GPAs of 2.75 or below. The number of accepted applicants exceeded the number of not-accepted applicants starting at a GPA between 3.75 and 4.0.

As is the case with the MCAT data, the GPA data in Figure 9.2 show that no undergraduate GPA ensures admission to medical school. Although applicants with total GPAs in the range of 3.50 to 3.75 were more likely to be accepted to medical school, a significant number of such applicants were not accepted. Again, these findings underscore the importance of other factors, such as personal characteristics and life experiences, in the medical student selection process.

Figure 9.2. Grade point average (GPA) total distribution, 2015 applicants.

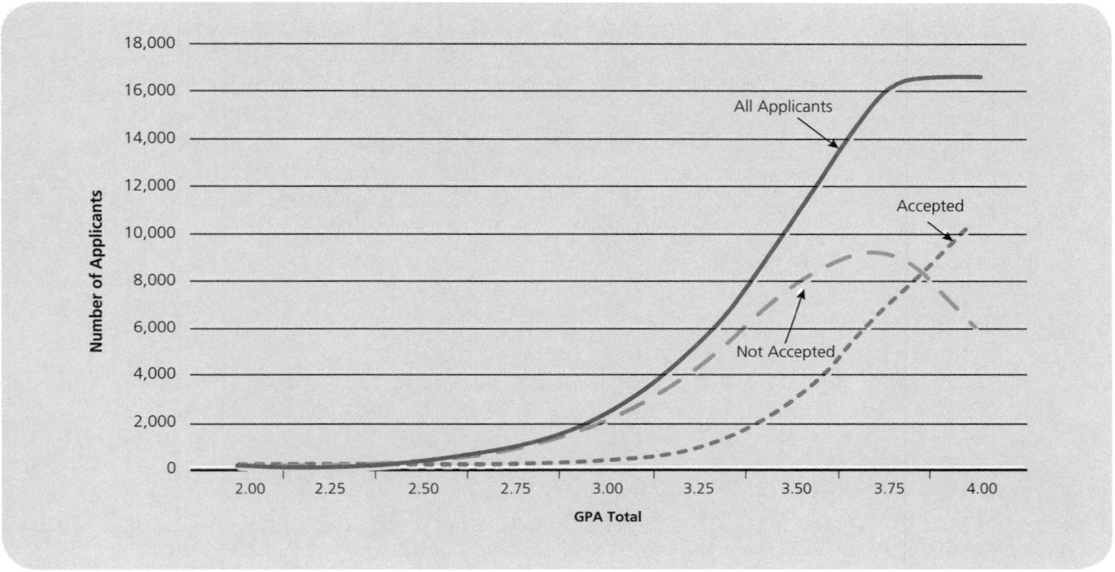

Source: AAMC Data Warehouse.

MCAT Score and Undergraduate GPA

Table 9.1 combines MCAT scores and undergraduate GPA for all applicants to medical school from 2013 to 2015. Note that these results are presented without regard to any of the other selection factors. If the data don't reflect your particular circumstances, please go to *www.aamc.org/data/facts* to see acceptance rates for specific demographic groups.

Table 9.1. MCAT Total Scores and Total GPAs of Applicants and Acceptees, 2013–2015 (Aggregated)

GPA Total	Acceptees (Accs), Applicants (Apps), and Percentage of Applicants Accepted	MCAT Total									
		3–14	15–17	18–20	21–23	24–26	27–29	30–32	33–35	36–38	39–45
3.80–4.00	Acceptees	2	7	44	326	1,394	4,293	7,401	6,635	3,962	1,433
	Applicants	71	190	546	1,647	3,755	7,448	9,997	8,031	4,548	1,586
	Accs/Apps	2.8%	3.7%	8.1%	19.8%	37.1%	57.6%	74.0%	82.6%	87.1%	90.4%
3.60–3.79	Acceptees	0	8	77	366	1,354	3,758	6,092	4,632	1,846	457
	Applicants	190	410	1,085	2,482	5,114	8,802	10,001	6,266	2,350	547
	Accs/Apps	0.0%	2.0%	7.1%	14.7%	26.5%	42.7%	60.9%	73.9%	78.6%	83.5%
3.40–3.59	Acceptees	1	11	55	305	989	2,244	3,623	2,377	833	160
	Applicants	340	572	1,361	2,781	4,889	7,336	7,794	3,944	1,204	221
	Accs/Apps	0.3%	1.9%	4.0%	11.0%	20.2%	30.6%	46.5%	60.3%	69.2%	72.4%
3.20–3.39	Acceptees	0	2	29	224	592	1,034	1,445	894	274	62
	Applicants	439	621	1,296	2,365	3,537	4,460	4,192	1,919	520	109
	Accs/Apps	0.0%	0.3%	2.2%	9.5%	16.7%	23.2%	34.5%	46.6%	52.7%	56.9%
3.00–3.19	Acceptees	0	2	25	117	354	456	521	284	104	18
	Applicants	415	610	995	1,582	2,292	2,373	1,868	814	250	40
	Accs/Apps	0.0%	0.3%	2.5%	7.4%	15.4%	19.2%	27.9%	34.9%	41.6%	45.0%
2.80–2.99	Acceptees	0	4	10	54	136	179	162	77	29	6
	Applicants	389	402	644	945	1,083	1,014	712	325	91	21
	Accs/Apps	0.0%	1.0%	1.6%	5.7%	12.6%	17.7%	22.8%	23.7%	31.9%	28.6%
2.60–2.79	Acceptees	0	1	11	20	50	55	52	40	12	4
	Applicants	299	280	392	485	536	397	270	132	50	12
	Accs/Apps	0.0%	0.4%	2.8%	4.1%	9.3%	13.9%	19.3%	30.3%	24.0%	33.3%
2.40–2.59	Acceptees	0	0	3	9	12	20	15	13	2	1
	Applicants	194	148	184	243	209	158	107	46	15	2
	Accs/Apps	0.0%	0.0%	1.6%	3.7%	5.7%	12.7%	14.0%	28.3%	13.3%	50.0%
2.20–2.39	Acceptees	0	0	0	0	8	6	12	1	1	0
	Applicants	137	98	98	96	85	68	51	16	7	2
	Accs/Apps	0.0%	0.0%	0.0%	0.0%	9.4%	8.8%	23.5%	6.3%	14.3%	0.0%
2.00–2.19	Acceptees	0	0	0	0	1	1	1	0	0	0
	Applicants	61	36	44	31	24	13	6	4	2	0
	Accs/Apps	0.0%	0.0%	0.0%	0.0%	4.2%	7.7%	16.7%	0.0%	0.0%	—
0.99–1.99	Acceptees	0	0	0	1	1	0	0	0	0	0
	Applicants	47	6	12	16	9	7	2	1	0	0
	Accs/Apps	0.0%	0.0%	0.0%	6.3%	11.1%	0.0%	0.0%	0.0%	—	—

Note: Percent accepted = ☐ <25%   ☐ 25%–49%   ▒ 50%–74%   ■ 75%–100%

Source: AAMC Data Warehouse: Applicant Matriculant File as of October 15, 2015.

Gender

Figure 9.3 presents information about the number and gender of the entire applicant pool and accepted applicants for the 1992 to 2015 entering classes. The largest annual applicant pool during the past 20 years was for the 2015 entering class, a pool of 52,550. The total for the 1996 entering class was 46,695, which until the 2013 pool of 48,014 was the largest applicant pool. In 2015, the applicant pool increased 6.2 percent from 2014.

The number of male applicants to the 2015 entering class increased by 1,473 from the number of male applicants to the previous year's entering class. The number of female applicants to the 2015 class increased by 1,589 over the number to the previous year's entering class. The year 2015 had the largest number of both male and female applicants on record.

Although the number of accepted applicants remained fairly constant for 10 years, it has started to increase in recent years, from a low of 17,312 in 1997 to a high of 21,647 in 2015. The number of accepted male applicants has fluctuated since 1992, with a low of 8,810 in 2003 and a high of 11,271 in 2015. The number of accepted female applicants has increased, with small fluctuations, from a low of 7,255 in the 1994 entering class to a high of 10,372 in 2015. The significant gaps between male and female applicants for the 1992 entering class (6,166) and the 1993 entering class (6,892) have lessened; 553 and 301 more women than men applied to the 2003 and 2004 entering classes, respectively. In 2005, 121 more men than women applied. In 2015, 3,320 more men than women applied to medical school. During the same time span, the gaps between accepted male and accepted female applicants decreased. Accepted male applicants outnumbered accepted female applicants by 2,951 for the 1992 entering class but only by 899 for the 2015 entering class.

The national ratio of male to female applicants was 49.2:50.8 for the 2003 entering class, the first time that the number of female applicants to medical school was greater than the number of male applicants. For the 2004 entering class, this trend continued, with a 49.6:50.4 ratio of male to female applicants. For the 2005 entering class, there were once again more male applicants than female applicants, with a male-to-female ratio of 50.2:49.8. This trend continued in 2015, with a ratio of male to female applicants of 53.2:46.8.

Figure 9.3. Applicants by gender and acceptance status, 1992–2015.

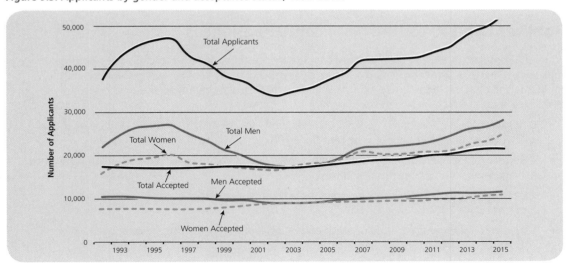

Source: AAMC Data Warehouse.

Age

Figure 9.4 shows that the age distribution for all applicants to the 2015 entering class was broad. The applicants between 21 and 28 years of age when they were expected to matriculate totaled 47,482; the number of applicants under 21 was 499; and applicants over 28 numbered 4,569. Figure 9.5 shows a similar finding for accepted applicants to the 2015 entering class; these individuals were between 18 and 54 years of age at the time of expected matriculation.

Figure 9.4. Age distribution, 2015 applicants.

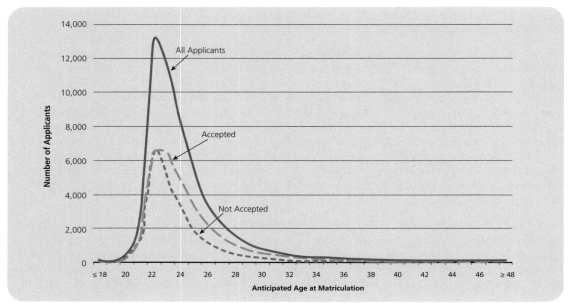

Source: AAMC Data Warehouse.

Applicant and Accepted Applicant Experiences

Figure 9.5 summarizes the volunteer and research experiences of AMCAS® applicants and accepted applicants to the 2015 entering class. The figure clearly shows the increase in the percentage of both applicants and accepted applicants reporting volunteer medical, community service, and research experience since 2002:

- 80 percent of accepted applicants reported community service and/or volunteer medical or clinical experience, an increase of about 4 percent since 2002

- 77 percent of applicants reported community service and/or volunteer medical or clinical experience, an increase of about 3 percent since 2002

- 82 percent of accepted applicants reported research and/or lab experience, an increase of about 13 percent since 2002

- 75 percent of applicants reported research and/or lab experience, an increase of about 12 percent since 2002

- 74 percent of accepted applicants reported nonmedical or nonclinical community service and/or volunteer experience, an increase of about 8 percent since 2002

- 70 percent of applicants reported nonmedical or nonclinical community service and/or volunteer experience, an increase of about 8 percent since 2002

Figure 9.5. Percentage of AMCAS applicants and accepted applicants reporting selected experiences.

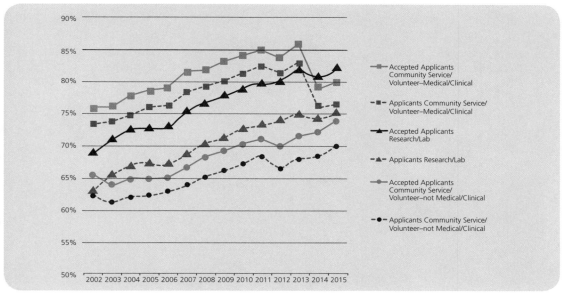

Source: AAMC Data Warehouse.

Self-Identity

Figure 9.6 shows self-reported race and ethnicity data for applicants to the 2013, 2014, and 2015 entering classes. Applicants can enter multiple races and ethnicities, so the sum of those shown does not equal the total number of applicants. Also, we couldn't include applicants for whom we have no race and ethnicity data. Additional information for applicants from groups underrepresented in medicine is available in Chapter 4.

Figure 9.6. Distribution of self-identity: All applicants, 2013–2015.*

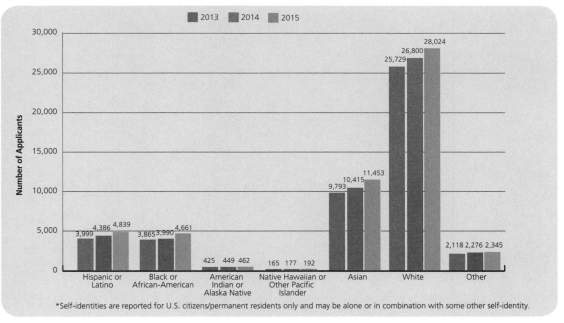

*Self-identities are reported for U.S. citizens/permanent residents only and may be alone or in combination with some other self-identity.

Source: AAMC Data Warehouse.

Chapter 10

You Can Afford Medical School

Juliet Siena Okoroh, MD
General Surgery Resident
University of California, San Francisco
University of California, San Diego
School of Medicine
Class of 2014

Medical school is expensive. Including the cost of tuition, fees, books, and living expenses, the average debt of a medical student in 2015 was $180,723. Fortunately, there are resources to help manage these expenses [see Figure 10.1]. Medical schools offer financial aid packages to students that may include federal loans, program-specific scholarships, and possibly grants. I chose my school partially because they offered me the most financial resources, which let me concentrate on being a student without worrying about how to pay my rent.

It is important to discuss your financial aid options. Ask about the average debt of graduating medical students, but understand that everyone's situation is unique. Consult with a financial aid officer or advisor before making any major decisions. Here are my personal debt management tips:
• Develop a good relationship with your financial aid counselor or financial aid office.
• Create a reasonable budget.
• Live within your means and track your expenses.
It's not always easy, but as you will learn in this chapter, there are many resources available to help you finance your medical education.

Building a Strong Financial Plan

You'll need to develop a strategy to cover the costs associated with your education. Don't let the numbers discourage you. There's help available.

When you look at the figures in Table 10.1, the financial challenges may seem overwhelming. Annual tuition, fees, and health insurance for the first year at state medical schools in 2014–2015 averaged about $33,107 for residents and $56,730 for nonresidents; at private schools, the average was $52,046 for residents and $53,653 for nonresidents.

According to recent surveys conducted by the AAMC, 86 percent of newly graduated MDs have medical school education loans, and 61 percent reported receiving some degree of help through scholarships, stipends, and grants (which you don't have to repay). So, it can be done, and it *is* … by tens of thousands of medical students every single year. But first: You'll need a plan.

Table 10.1. Tuition, Fees, and Health Insurance for 2015–2016 First-Year Students in U.S. Medical Schools* **(in Dollars)**

Private Schools

Student Category	Range	Median	Average
Resident	$21,950–$63,321	$55,259	$53,917
Nonresident	$35,050–$64,858	$56,702	$55,345

Public Schools

Student Category	Range	Median	Average
Resident	$0**–$50,648	$35,223	$33,793
Nonresident	$22,113–$91,061	$60,437	$58,212

*Analysis excludes the Brody School of Medicine at East Carolina University, University of Massachusetts Medical School, Mercer University School of Medicine, University of Mississippi School of Medicine, and Southern Illinois School of Medicine. These schools do not accept nonresident medical students, and therefore, they do not report nonresident tuition and fees. Public schools excludes Uniformed Services University of Health Sciences, which does not charge tuition or student fees.

**Instead of paying tuition and fees, students at Uniformed Services–Hebert incur a national service obligation.

Source: 2015–2016 AAMC Tuition and Student Fees Questionnaire.

Before you actually borrow money, it's important that you understand—and adhere to—the basic principles of successful money management. With that in mind, the two basic recommendations that follow should help you build a strong financial foundation.

1. Live Within Your Means

All other efforts to "afford" medical school and handle your monies wisely will be undermined if you don't have a plan of action for your finances. Having a spending plan is the cornerstone of a solid financial foundation. Let's face it, money will be tight during medical school, and a realistic spending plan will be critical to your financial well-being. A well-crafted plan will help you maintain better control of your spending, ensure you cover your essential expenses, and prepare you for unexpected expenses by building an emergency fund.

Creating a budget involves only a few steps:

- Income—document incoming funds, which will likely be in the form of student loans

- Expenses—identify outgoing expenses, like rent, food, and tuition

- Discretionary income—calculate your discretionary income to see if your spending plan allows you to live within your means

- For assistance in creating a realistic budget, contact the financial aid office of the medical school you're interested in attending. Often, they can provide some approximations of the average amount

Figure 10.1. Distribution of financial aid among medical students.

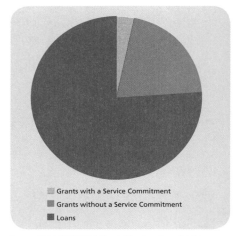

- Grants with a Service Commitment
- Grants without a Service Commitment
- Loans

Source: 2014–2015 LCME Part I-B Student Financial Aid Questionnaire.

of student loan monies available to live on and the expected costs of necessities while attending medical school.

2. Manage Your Debt Wisely

Your Total Income − **Your Total Expenses** = **Your Discretionary Income**

- Given the costs of medical school, it's understandable that the vast majority of medical students borrow money to fund their education—and, as of 2015, graduate with median education debt of $183,000. The ability to manage debt wisely is important, regardless of one's situation, and it becomes even more critical for you—a prospective medical student—when you consider the degree to which you're likely to rely on loans to help pay for your education.

- Be conscious of the amount you're likely to borrow, and be comfortable knowing that your future income will allow you to repay your student loan debt.

- Educate yourself about various financing possibilities before you arrive at medical school, and diligently search for free money, such as scholarships, grants, and repayment assistance programs.

- Understand your responsibilities—beyond making payments—that come with borrowing student loans. These include knowing what loans you borrowed, where to send payments, and when payments are due. You'll also be responsible for notifying your servicers of any changes to your name, contact information, or enrollment status.

- Stay organized. Maintain accurate financial aid records, copies of application forms, and any related paperwork. This also means opening and reading all mail pertaining to your student loan debt. The Medloans® Organizer and Calculator is a tool that can help you keep everything organized. Every accepted medical school student is given access to this tool, found at *www.aamc.org/first*.

- Build a good credit score by meeting your financial obligations. In doing so, you'll strengthen your ability to qualify for and obtain attractive interest rates for credit-based loans, land a job, and rent an apartment. For more information, go to *www.aamc.org/first/creditscore*.

- There's an abundance of resources to help you through this process—including those provided by your pre-health advisor, the pages that follow in this book, and the AAMC's Financial Information, Resources, Services, and Tools (FIRST) program. FIRST provides a wide range of resources to help medical school applicants and students make smart decisions about student loans, effectively manage their education debt, and expand their financial skills. The AAMC also provides financial management assistance through a free financial literacy program called SALT. SALT provides practical information on budgeting, money management, credit, debt management, and more. Sign up for your free SALT account at *www.saltmoney.org/AAMCpremed*.

- The financial aid package offered by each medical school may be a significant factor when you're deciding which offer to accept. For information on this and other considerations, see Chapter 6, "Choosing the Schools That Are Right for You."

3. Make Sure You're "Choosing Your Schools"

- Some medical schools require a credit history as part of the financial aid application and require that applicants resolve any credit problems before they matriculate. Some medical schools will grant a delay of matriculation to an accepted applicant who must address credit problems. Applicants are advised to contact financial aid offices at the medical schools they're interested in to discuss financial aid eligibility and, if necessary, resolve any outstanding credit problems.

Tips to Help Your Credit Score

- Pay your bills on time.

- Limit your credit accounts.

- Keep balances below your credit limit and pay off debt.

- Pay down debt whenever possible.

- Make sure you are current on all outstanding credit obligations.

- Check your credit report regularly at *www.annualcreditreport.com*.

Types of Financial Aid

How Will You Pay for Medical School?

First, remember that you're not alone. While the ultimate financial responsibility for your medical education rests with you and your family, there are many resources and tools to help you. The financial aid officer at your medical school will assist you, but you'll also want to talk to your pre-health advisor and familiarize yourself with the Financial Aid Fact Sheets on the AAMC FIRST website (*www.aamc.org/first*). For example, see Figure 10.2. Financial aid typically available to medical students includes loans, grants, and scholarships (see Table 10.2).

Figure 10.2. Medical student education debt, cost, and loan repayment fact card.

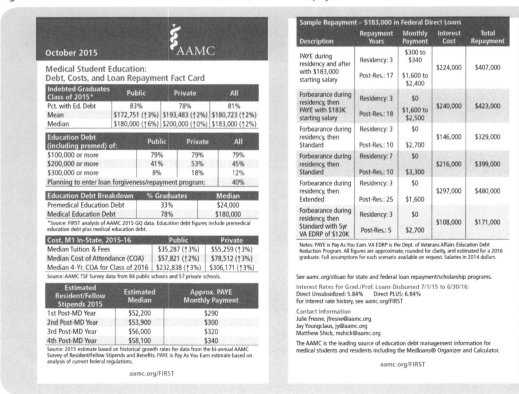

Table 10.2. Federal Student Loans for Medical Students

Characteristics	Direct Unsubsidized Loan	Direct PLUS Loan	Loans for Disadvantaged Students	Primary Care Loan
Lender	The federal government	The federal government	Medical school financial aid office on behalf of the Department of HHS	Medical school financial aid office on behalf of the Department of HHS
Based on Need	No	No	Yes[1]	Yes[2]
Citizenship Requirement	U.S. citizen, U.S. national, or U.S. permanent resident	U.S. citizen, U.S. national, or U.S. permanent resident	U.S. citizen, U.S. national, or U.S. permanent resident	U.S. citizen, U.S. national, or U.S. permanent resident
Borrowing Limits	$40,500–$47,167/year, $224,000 cumulative maximum for pre-med and medical borrowing[3]	Annual cost of attendance minus other financial aid	Up to cost of attendance (third- and fourth-year students may receive additional funds to repay previous educational loans received while attending medical school)[3]	Up to cost of attendance (third- and fourth-year students may receive additional funds to repay previous educational loans received while attending medical school)[3]
Interest Rate	For loans disbursed after July 1, 2013, the rate is fixed for the life of the loan. These fixed rates are calculated every July 1st and are effective for loans disbursed during the next academic year. For current rates, visit *studentaid.ed.gov/types/loans/interest-rates.*	For loans disbursed after July 1, 2013, the rate is fixed for the life of the loan. These fixed rates are calculated every July 1st and are effective for loans disbursed during the next academic year. For current rates, visit *studentaid.ed.gov/types/loans/interest-rates.*	5%	5%
Interest Subsidy	No	No	While in school, deferment, and grace period	While in school, deferment, and grace period
Grace Period	6 months	None	1 year	1 year
Deferments	While in school and other possible deferment periods based on eligibility (check your promissory note or ask your financial aid officer)	While in school and 6 months after separating from school (post-enrollment deferment)	While in school and during approved eligible activities	While in school and during a primary care residency (check your promissory note or ask your financial aid officer)
Repayment Requirements	Repayment plans and postponement options exist during residency and beyond	Repayment plans and postponement options exist during residency and beyond	Minimum: $40/month; 10 to 25 years to repay, at the discretion of the institution; may be eligible for federal loan consolidation	Minimum: $40/month; 10 to 25 years to repay; not eligible for loan consolidation
Prepayment Penalties	None			
Allowable Cancellations	Death or total and permanent disability			

[1] Parent financial information is required for consideration for dependent students.
[2] Borrower must agree upon signing loan agreement to enter and complete a primary care residency and practice in a primary care field, which together must be a total of 10 years in length or until the loan is repaid in full, whichever occurs first. Parent financial information is required for consideration for dependent students.
[3] Both annual and aggregate maximums are subject to change, pending congressional action.

Loans

It's likely that your primary financial funding for medical school will come from federal student loans—a form of financial aid. They are normally the first type of loan suggested, before you consider private loans. Table 10.2 provides specific information about four of the most common federal loans used by medical students:

- Direct Unsubsidized Loans

- Direct PLUS Loans

- Loans for Disadvantaged Students (LDS)

- Primary Care Loans (PCL)

Medical school is expensive; however, physicians' salaries are excellent. For example, in 2014, the median starting salary for a family practice physician was $187,298 (according to the *Medical Group Management Association (MGMA) Physician Placement Starting Salary Survey 2015 Report*, based on 2014 data). Most other specialties have even higher starting salaries.

Grants and Scholarships

When it comes to financing your medical education, the best money is free money, often referred to as "gift aid," which you don't have to repay. While grants and scholarships are likely to cover only a portion of your overall educational costs, it's worth noting that many students get some degree of funding from these sources. The source of gift aid can be from the federal government, the state government, other outside resources, and your medical school. Your medical school financial aid officer is the best source of information about which grants and scholarships may be available to you.

The Financial Aid Application Process

The financial aid process may vary slightly by institution, so you'll want to discuss each school's requirements with the financial aid officer. Generally, most schools require that you're a U.S. citizen or permanent resident, that you're making satisfactory academic progress, and that you're in compliance with Selective Service registration requirements.

Regardless of the medical school, there's a standard process for applying for federal financial aid.

Step 1. Fill Out the FAFSA

Completing the Free Application for Federal Student Aid (FAFSA) is the first step toward getting federal aid for medical school. Completing the FAFSA online is easy and free. Some schools may require that you provide parental financial information on the FAFSA or through a supplemental application. The schools listed on your FAFSA will receive your financial information to then determine your eligibility for aid.

Step 2. Investigate Other Sources of Aid

Contact the financial aid offices at the medical schools you're interested in to investigate other sources of institutional aid, such as loans, scholarships, and grants.

Step 3. Receive and Reply to the Award Letter

Once your FAFSA and other required forms are received and processed by a medical school's financial aid office, you'll receive an award letter indicating the types and amounts of financial aid you qualify for—along with directions for accepting or declining the aid. Be sure to follow the instructions to receive your financial aid in a timely manner. For more information on award letters, review the Award Letter Fact Sheet: *students-residents.aamc.org/financial-aid/article/what-is-an-award-letter.*

When awarding aid, each financial aid office has principles that are guided by multiple factors. The aid package is determined by eligibility for federal aid, available institutional resources, family resources, and the institution's mission. Additionally, the school compares the cost of attendance and other external variables before making a final determination of aid eligibility. For eligibility and additional details, talk with the financial aid officer at the medical school you plan to attend.

How Medical Schools Determine Eligibility for Financial Aid

Medical schools are sensitive to the financial needs of students. Guided by federal regulations, the financial aid officer will determine your aid eligibility by examining the following questions.

How much does it cost?

The cost of medical education includes tuition, fees, books, supplies, equipment, and living expenses. These components make up the school's cost of attendance (COA) and vary by school. (You can find out the tuition and fees and COA of each medical school on the Medical School Admission Requirements website, *www.aamc.org/msar.*)

What are your resources?

The next area that will be calculated is the amount you'll be required to pay toward the cost of the education. This amount, called the expected family contribution (EFC), is determined through a need-analysis formula to ensure that all students are treated equitably. Both income and assets are considered.

Even though you're considered independent for purposes of federal loans, many institutions require parental financial information to determine eligibility for institutional grants, scholarships, and school-based loans. School officials use this information to assess the student's ability to pay rather than willingness to pay, helping ensure that certain types of aid are awarded to students with the greatest need.

What additional resources are needed?

Finally, the financial aid office will subtract your EFC from the institution's total cost of attendance. The remainder determines how much aid you'll need for the upcoming academic year. At this point, the medical school will send you an "award letter" detailing the amount and type of financial aid available to you.

You'll be asked to accept or decline the offer (or a portion of it) and return the letter to the school. (The amount of financial aid an institution offers may be an important factor in choosing which school to attend. See Chapter 6 for additional information and guidance on making your selection. To further assist you in the analysis of your award letters, all accepted applicants are given complimentary access to the Medloans Organizer and Calculator [*www.aamc.org/medloans*]. This tool can be used to clearly see the total cost associated with the financing options provided in the award letters.)

Forgiveness and Repayment Assistance Programs

Loan forgiveness and repayment programs are available for students interested in reducing their education loan debt through service. These are great options if your career goals align with those of the particular repayment or forgiveness program. The programs vary in structure, requirements, and award amounts.

The federal government provides both service commitment and loan repayment benefits to medical students interested in pursuing careers in primary care and to those committed to working in medically underserved areas.

Additionally, the federal grovernment has a loan forgiveness program to reward borrowers who choose to work in public service, and borrowers also currently have the option of some repayment plans offering loan forgiveness if a balance still remains at the end of their loan term.

Some state programs are available to students and graduates in return for a commitment to serve in the state's areas of need. Review the Loan Repayment/Forgiveness and Scholarship Programs database at *www.aamc.org/stloan*.

The U.S. Armed Forces have programs that offer support to students enrolled in civilian medical schools in exchange for service in the branch that provided the funding.

Federal Loans and Repayment

The benefits available with the federal student loan programs include these:

For additional details on service commitment and loan forgiveness, please see Repayment Assistance Through Forgiveness, Scholarships, or Service on the FIRST website at *www.aamc.org/first.*

- **Peace of mind.** Payments are not required until after medical school is over. Payments can even be postponed throughout residency, if a borrower doesn't want to make payments during that time.

- **Fixed interest rates.** Rates will not rise, and interest rate reductions may even be available if borrowers elect automatic electronic payment and/or make their payments on time.

- **Various repayment plans.** Flexible plans are available to make payments affordable—even during residency.

- **Education tax credits or deductions.** Some borrowers may be eligible for tax benefits; consult Publication 970 from the IRS for more information (*www.irs.gov/pub/irs-pdf/p970.pdf*).

As you near graduation, your financial aid office and your loan servicers will supply the details you need to successfully manage your debt after graduation. To learn more, check out FIRST's Financial Aid Fact Sheets on loan repayment options at *www.aamc.org/first*.

A Final Word About Financing Your Medical Education

The AAMC has a variety of financial information, resources, services, and tools for students and residents interested in learning about debt management. You're encouraged to use the resources at *www.aamc .org/first* to help you accomplish your financial goals.

Service Commitment and Loan Forgiveness Programs

Learn more about these programs at the websites listed below, and review FIRST's Consumer and Federal Financial Aid Resources webpage at *students-residents.aamc.org/financial-aid/article/resources*:

Army: *www.goarmy.com/amedd/hpsp.html*

Air Force: *www.airforce.com/opportunities/healthcare/education*

National Health Service Corps: *www.nhsc.hrsa.gov/index.html*

NIH Loan Repayment: *www.lrp.nih.gov/index.aspx*

Navy: *www.navy.com/careers/healthcare/physicians/*

Public Service Programs: *studentaid.ed.gov/sa/repay-loans/forgiveness-cancellation/public-service*

State and Federal Programs: *www.aamc.org/stloan*

 Worksheets at the end of chapters in this guide are available in fillable PDF format at *www.aamc.org/msar-resources.*

INCOME:

Salary (after deductions) _____

Spouse salary (after deductions) _____

Investment income _____

Financial aid (in excess of tuition and fees) _____

Gifts _____

Income tax refunds _____

Other _____

Veteran's benefits _____

Total Income _____

FIXED EXPENSES:

Tuition and fees _____

Books and supplies _____

Regular savings _____

Rent/mortgage _____

Utilities* _____

Telephone (base rate) _____

Taxes (federal, state) _____

Vehicle payments _____

Other transportation _____

Credit card payments _____

Personal loans _____

Educational loans _____

Insurance (life and health) _____

Home/renter insurance _____

Auto insurance _____

Auto registration/taxes _____

Professional fees/dues _____

Child care _____

Other _____

Total Fixed Expenses _____

VARIABLE OR FLEXIBLE EXPENSES:

Food/household supplies _____

Dining Out _____

Clothes _____

Laundry/dry cleaning _____

Gas, oil, auto maintenance _____

Parking _____

Medical/dental/eye care _____

Hobbies/recreation _____

Entertainment _____

Travel/vacation _____

Pets, supplies, food _____

Sports _____

CDs and books _____

Health and beauty aids _____

Haircuts _____

Postage _____

Subscriptions _____

Cable TV _____

Cell phone _____

Gifts _____

Charity/contributions _____

Other _____

Total Variable Expenses _____

Total Fixed Expenses + _____

Total Monthly Expenses = _____

Total Income _____

Less Total Monthly Expenses – _____

Total Discretionary Income = _____
(or Deficit)

*Gas, electric, water, sewer, garbage.

Pre-Med Worksheet from the *Official Guide to Medical School Admissions*
Association of American Medical Colleges

Chapter 11

Undergraduate/MD Programs

Stephanie K. Napolitano, MD, MPH
Pediatrics Resident
Nationwide Children's Hospital
Case Western Reserve University
Class of 2015

I was fortunate to attend a high school that balanced academic rigor and a personal life, and I wondered if I'd be able to find this balance in medical school. I learned about BS/MD programs during a college interview. It sounded like the perfect way to achieve the balance I was looking for— four years of undergraduate studies, no required major, the option to take the MCAT® exam and apply elsewhere or forego the stress and remain at the same university for medical school.

If you are a high school student dedicated to pursuing medicine, consider the combined college/MD programs. Programs range in length from six to nine years. During the initial two to four years, students complete their premedical coursework and earn their bachelor's degree. During the subsequent four years, students learn in a traditional medical school setting. These programs provide students with advantages including a faster education track, freedom from application stress, and liberation from the daunting MCAT exam. It's not for everyone, but if it's something you're considering, this chapter will give you a list of BS/MD programs.

Although about 91 percent of students focus solely on obtaining their MD, about 3.1 percent graduate from joint bachelor's/MD programs, and 3.2 percent earn a joint MD/PhD, according to the AAMC's 2015 Graduation Questionnaire (GQ).

Purposes of These Programs

The purposes of these programs vary by institution and include the following:

- To permit highly qualified students to plan and complete a broad liberal arts education before starting their medical studies

- To attract highly capable students to the sponsoring medical school

- To enhance diversity in the educational environment

- To reduce the total number of years required to complete the MD degree

- To educate physicians likely to practice in particular geographic areas or work with medically underserved populations

- To reduce the costs of a medical education

- To prepare physician-scientists and future leaders in health policy

Potential applicants should familiarize themselves with the mission and statement of goals of each combined degree program in which they have an interest to ensure an appropriate match between their educational and professional goals and those of the program.

These programs typically represent relationships between a medical school and one or more undergraduate colleges located in the same geographic region. They are sometimes part of the same university system, or they can be independent institutions.

Admission is open to highly qualified, mature high school students who are committed to a future career in medicine. Some of these programs are also open to college freshmen and sophomores. For more information, see the Medical School Admission Requirements website, specifically the Application Requirements section for BS/MD programs (*www.aamc.org/msar*). State-supported schools generally admit few out-of-state applicants to their combined college/MD programs; private schools tend to have greater flexibility about state of residency.

While academic requirements vary among the schools sponsoring these programs, they typically include biology, chemistry, physics, English, mathematics, and social science courses. Calculus and foreign-language courses are also frequently required; a computer science course is sometimes recommended. Admission to the MD portion of the program may occur immediately or after a student completes a prescribed number of semesters with a minimum grade point average (GPA). In some programs, students are not required to take the MCAT exam; in other programs, a minimum MCAT score must be attained to progress through the program.

Progressing through the program from the undergraduate to the medical curricula is usually contingent on a student's achieving specific criteria in terms of standardized test scores, GPAs, and meeting the school's expectations for personal and professional behavior.

If you're a high school student interested in a combined undergraduate/MD program, you should consult your high school guidance counselor to ensure that you're enrolled in a challenging college preparatory curriculum, one that incorporates the specific courses required for admission to the program. The program descriptions in the Medical School Admission Requirements website were compiled from medical schools sponsoring programs of interest to high school students. For more information about the Medical School Admission Requirements website, a preview of the site, and a complete list of site features, data, and information, see *www.aamc.org/msar*. If you're a college freshman or sophomore interested in these programs, please speak with your school's pre-health advisor. For additional information about specific programs, contact each school directly.

View the alphabetical list of the combined undergraduate/MD programs by state or the list by number of years to complete them in this chapter, or see detailed individual profiles of the programs on the Medical School Admission Requirements website.

Medical Schools Offering Combined Undergraduate/MD Programs, by State, 2015–2016

Alabama
University of Alabama School of Medicine

University of South Alabama College of Medicine

Connecticut
University of Connecticut and University of Connecticut School of Medicine

Delaware
University of Delaware

District of Columbia
George Washington University School of Medicine and Health Sciences and Columbian College of Arts and Sciences

Howard University College of Medicine

Florida
University of Florida College of Medicine

University of Miami Leonard M. Miller School of Medicine

Illinois
Northwestern University The Feinberg School of Medicine

University of Illinois College of Medicine

Massachusetts
Boston University School of Medicine

Michigan
Wayne State University School of Medicine

Missouri
Saint Louis University School of Medicine

University of Missouri—Kansas City School of Medicine

Washington University in St. Louis School of Medicine

Nevada
University of Nevada School of Medicine

New Jersey
Rutgers, New Jersey Medical School 7-Year BA/MD Program

Rutgers, New Jersey Medical School BA/MD Program

Rutgers, Robert Wood Johnson Medical School BA/MD Program

New Mexico
University of New Mexico School of Medicine

New York

Brooklyn College and SUNY Downstate Medical Center College of Medicine

Rensselaer Polytechnic Institute and Albany Medical College

SUNY Upstate Medical University Hobart William Smith College Blackwell Medical Scholarship Program

Siena College and Albany Medical College

Sophie Davis School of Biomedical Education at the City College of New York

St. Bonaventure University and George Washington University School of Medicine and Health Sciences

Stony Brook University and Stony Brook University School of Medicine

Union College and Albany Medical College

University of Rochester School of Medicine and Dentistry

Ohio

Case Western Reserve University School of Medicine

Northeast Ohio Medical University

University of Cincinnati College of Medicine

Pennsylvania

Drexel University and Drexel University College of Medicine

Lehigh University and Drexel University College of Medicine

Pennsylvania State University and Sidney Kimmel Medical College at Jefferson University

Temple University School of Medicine

Villanova University and Drexel University College of Medicine

Puerto Rico

MD Binary Program of Pontifical Catholic University of Puerto Rico and Ponce School of Medicine and Health Sciences

Rhode Island

The Warren Alpert Medical School of Brown University

Tennessee

Fisk University and Meharry Medical College

Texas

Baylor University and Baylor College of Medicine (Baylor 2 Medical Track)

Houston Premedical Academy and Baylor College of Medicine

Premedical Honors College, University of Texas Rio Grande Valley (UTRGV)

Rice University and Baylor College of Medicine

University of Texas School of Medicine at San Antonio

Virginia

Eastern Virginia Medical School

Virginia Commonwealth University School of Medicine

Medical Schools Offering Combined Undergraduate/MD Programs, by Number of Years, 2015–2016

6 Years

University of Missouri—Kansas City School of Medicine

6–7 Years

Northeast Ohio Medical University

Pennsylvania State University and Sidney Kimmel Medical College at Jefferson Medical College

University of Miami Leonard M. Miller School of Medicine

7 Years

Boston University School of Medicine (8-year option available)

Drexel University and Drexel University College of Medicine

Fisk University and Meharry Medical College

George Washington University School of Medicine and Health Sciences and Columbian School of Arts and Sciences

Lehigh University and Drexel University College of Medicine

Northwestern University Feinberg School of Medicine

Rensselaer Polytechnic Institute and Albany Medical College

Rutgers, New Jersey Medical School BA/MD Program

Rutgers, Robert Wood Johnson Medical School

Sophie Davis School of Biomedical Education at the City College of New York

University of Florida College of Medicine

University of Illinois College of Medicine

University of Nevada School of Medicine

University of Texas School of Medicine at San Antonio

Villanova University and Drexel University College of Medicine

8 Years

Baylor University and Baylor College of Medicine (Baylor 2 Medical Track)

Brooklyn College and SUNY Downstate Medical Center College of Medicine

Case Western Reserve University School of Medicine

Eastern Virginia Medical School

Hobart and William Smith Colleges and SUNY Upstate Medical University

Houston Premedical Academy and Baylor College of Medicine

Howard University College of Medicine

Premedical Honors College, Baylor College of Medicine (BCM) and University of Texas Rio Grande Valley (UTRGV)

Rice University and Baylor College of Medicine

Rutgers New Jersey Medical School

Rutgers, Robert Wood Johnson Medical School

Saint Louis University School of Medicine

Siena College and Albany Medical College

St. Bonaventure University and George Washington University School of Medicine and Health Sciences

Stony Brook University and Stony Brook University School of Medicine

Union College and Albany Medical College

University of Alabama School of Medicine

University of California, San Diego School of Medicine

University of Cincinnati College of Medicine

University of Connecticut and University of Connecticut School of Medicine

University of New Mexico School of Medicine

University of Rochester School of Medicine and Dentistry

University of South Alabama College of Medicine

University of Southern California College of Letters, Arts, and Sciences and Keck School of Medicine

Virginia Commonwealth University School of Medicine

Warren Alpert Medical School of Brown University

Wayne State University School of Medicine

Wilkes University and SUNY Upstate Medical University

9 Years
University of Cincinnati College of Medicine (College of Engineering—undergraduate)

 Worksheets at the end of chapters in this guide are available in fillable PDF format at *www.aamc.org/msar-resources*.

1. **Name of BS/MD Program** _____

Why interested in this program: _____

# of Years: _____   Accepts out-of-state? _____   Application deadline: _____

When eligible to apply: College freshman ___   High school senior ___   Other _____

2. **Name of BS/MD Program** _____

Why interested in this program: _____

# of Years: _____   Accepts out-of-state? _____   Application deadline: _____

When eligible to apply: College freshman ___   High school senior ___   Other _____

3. **Name of BS/MD Program** _____

Why interested in this program: _____

# of Years: _____   Accepts out-of-state? _____   Application deadline: _____

When eligible to apply: College freshman ___   High school senior ___   Other _____

4. **Name of BS/MD Program** _____

Why interested in this program: _____

# of Years: _____   Accepts out-of-state? _____   Application deadline: _____

When eligible to apply: College freshman ___   High school senior ___   Other _____

Chapter 12

MD/PhD Programs

As a science major, I developed an interest in research as a way to engage in the process of discovery and innovation, ask new questions, and apply the technical knowledge I had been acquiring. I find becoming immersed in the question of how things work while testing hypotheses about how to improve the pathophysiology of disease is extremely rewarding.

The rigor and intellectual stimulation of the research process engages and energizes me; however, I have always been drawn to the bedside. The process of developing a connection with a patient, investigating his or her illness or disease, and offering relief for their suffering is immensely gratifying and meaningful.

Catherine Spina, MD, PhD
Intern, Mount Auburn Hospital
Department of Medicine
Resident, Columbia University
Department of Radiation Oncology
Boston University School of Medicine
Class of 2015

In the laboratory, I can create, discover, and innovate with the long- term goal of impacting how we care for whole patient populations. While in the clinic, my impact as a physician is immediate. Being unable to choose between science and medicine, I chose to pursue both through the MD/PhD program. This is ideal for me because it supports my goal of translating basic research into clinical solutions and allows my clinical experience to inform and guide my research.

The Education of a Physician-Scientist

Although about 90 percent of students are solely enrolled in an MD program, about 3 percent earn a joint MD/PhD, 3 percent graduate from joint bachelor's/MD programs, and 2 percent earn a dual MD/MPH or MD/MBA degree.

Physician-scientists—those who are trained in both medicine and research—are greatly needed in today's world. There is a synergy that results when experimental thinking and clinical practice are joined, and that combination is found among those who have completed both MD and PhD degrees. These individuals help translate the achievements of basic research into active clinical practice and, in doing so, strengthen the link between medical knowledge and research as they prevent, diagnose, and treat disease. If this is the path you prefer, you'll enjoy a busy, challenging, and rewarding career.

Advantages of the MD/PhD Dual Degree

One route to a career as a physician-scientist is enrollment in a combined MD/PhD program. Although you can complete a PhD program before or after receiving your MD degree, there are several advantages to pursuing joint MD/PhD education:

- The greatest advantage of the dual-degree program is the integration of research and clinical training. This integrated approach may include seminars that cross departments and interactions with teams composed of both basic science and clinical investigators.

- You can save a significant amount of time. Most MD/PhD programs can be completed in seven or eight years, compared with the nine or more years it would take to earn both degrees independently.

- Students in MD/PhD programs have access to opportunities for research and faculty mentoring to an extent frequently unavailable to MD-only students. As a result, these students are often able to enhance their mastery of the basic science needed to identify patients' underlying clinical problems and, ultimately, use that information to develop improvements in diagnosis and treatment. To learn more about available programs and how to apply, go to *www.aamc.org/mdphd*.

Paths to a Research Career

If you're interested in a career in research but you aren't sure whether you want to pursue a dual MD/PhD degree, here are some other options you can explore:

- **PhD in Biomedical Sciences.** You can earn a PhD in biomedical sciences in graduate programs at medical schools. The program typically includes one or two years of core coursework, lab rotations to select a mentor, and three to four years of doctoral research. To learn more about available programs and how to apply, go to *www.aamc.org/phd*.

> ### Professional School Fair—MD/PhD: Is It Right for Me?
>
> In this videocast, the leaders of medical school MD/PhD programs describe undergraduate preparation and application processes and discuss training in MD/PhD programs and postgraduate career opportunities: *videocast.nih.gov/Summary. asp?File=15209&bhcp=1*.

- **MS Degree or Certificate in Clinical Research.** You might also consider graduate work leading to a master's degree or certificate in clinical research. These programs, which can be pursued jointly or after receiving your PhD or MD, are offered at many medical schools and graduate schools throughout the country.

- **"Year-Enrichment" Program.** Another option is to take a year away from your MD program to conduct research under the direction of a mentor in a scholars program. Three such programs are the **Fogarty International Clinical Research Scholarship Program**, the **National Institutes of Health (NIH) Medical Research Scholars Program**, and the **Howard Hughes Medical Institute (HHMI) Research Fellows Program**. For details, see *www.fogartyscholars.org*, *www.cc.nih.gov/training/mrsp/ index.html*, and *www.hhmi.org/grants/individuals/medical-fellows/*. In addition, many medical schools offer similar opportunities for their students.

Research Specialties

Like their PhD-only counterparts, people who hold a combined degree can pursue many scientific specialties. Most students earn their PhDs in biomedical disciplines such as biochemistry, biomedical engineering, biophysics, cell biology, genetics, immunology, microbiology, neuroscience, and pharmacology.

It's important to know, however, that not every research specialty is offered at every medical school and that curricula can vary from institution to institution. In some schools, for example, MD/PhD students complete their graduate work in the social sciences or humanities—fields of study outside laboratory disciplines—in areas such as anthropology, computational biology, economics, engineering, health care policy, mathematics, physics, and sociology.

To learn more, go to *students-residents.aamc.org/choosing-medical-career/article/md-phd-social-sciences-or-humanities-it-right-me/*.

View a summary of MD/PhD programs and graduate fields of study at */aamc-orange.global.ssl.fastly.net/ production/media/filer_public/71/8b/718bcf9f-21a3-4d77-9423-a2fce84408f1/faqtable.pdf*.

Clinical Specialties

MD/PhD students can pursue any of many clinical specialties. The clinical specialty choices of students graduating from MD/Ph.D. programs over the past five years indicate strong interest in internal medicine, pathology, and pediatrics.

Compared with MD-only graduates, MD/PhD graduates are more likely to enter residencies in radiation oncology, child neurology, and pathology and less likely to go into family medicine, emergency medicine, and obstetrics/gynecology. Additionally, the majority of dual-degree students enter residencies after graduation. A small percentage of program graduates who do not enter residency typically go straight into a research postdoctoral fellowship position.

The Typical Program

Almost all U.S. and Canadian medical schools have MD/PhD programs in one or more areas of specialization. (You can search for MD/PhD programs on the Medical School Admission Requirements website and view a listing of MD/PhD programs available at AAMC-member medical schools at *students-residents.aamc.org/applying-medical-school/article/applying-mdphd-programs-2/*.) Some programs are relatively small (one or two new students each year, with a total of a dozen or so students), and others are much larger (up to 25 new students annually and a total enrollment of around 190).

Although there are differences among programs, core elements are common to almost all. The typical program is completed in seven to eight years and includes the following:

- Completion of the first two years of combined medical and graduate school coursework

- Three to five years of doctoral research, including the completion of a thesis project

- A return to medical school for core clinical training and electives during the final years of the medical curriculum

At most schools, integrated approaches to graduate and medical education have been introduced throughout the curricula, quite extensively in some programs. In addition, most programs engage students in a wide range of other activities to enrich their training experience.

Residency Programs After Graduation

After medical school, most MD/PhD students transition to residencies just like a traditional medical student. Several residencies around the country offer highly structured programs in which research is fully integrated into clinical training. They differ in their overall composition but generally offer a shortened residency training period. For more information, visit *students-residents.aamc.org/choosing-medical-career/article/career-paths-md-phd-graduate*s.

Application and Admission

Nearly all MD/PhD programs participate in the American Medical College Application Service® (AMCAS®) application process described in Chapter 7.

If you choose to pursue the dual-degree program, you'll designate yourself as a combined MD/PhD training applicant and complete two additional essays: one explaining why you are interested in the joint training program and the other describing your research experience. Specifics in the application process—and the prerequisites required for admission—vary from school to school. (Some institutions, for example, require GRE scores.) For complete information about a dual-degree program that interests you, review the program description at the appropriate medical school's website.

Where Physician-Scientists Work

About 75 percent of MD/PhD graduates are employed as faculty members in academic medical centers or in pharmaceutical companies. Other graduates work in a wide range of other capacities, including as scientists in biotechnology firms, the federal government, clinical medicine, and basic research.

Source: LF Brass, et al. Are MD-PhD programs meeting their goals? An analysis of career choices made by graduates of 24 MD-PhD programs. Academic Medicine 2010; 85(4):692–701.

Factors Considered by Admission Committees

Admission committee members will review the application materials for the usual experiences, attributes, and metrics that are important for admitting students to MD-only programs (see Chapter 8). But because MD/PhD applicants plan to become both physicians and scientists, committee members will also look for evidence of an applicant's passion and aptitude for research. They accomplish this largely through review of an applicant's statement of career goals and in letters of evaluation from faculty or researchers with whom the applicant has worked. In particular, committee members seek confirmation of these things:

- Relevant and substantive research experience during or after college

- An appreciation for and understanding of the work of physician-scientists

- Intellectual drive, research ability, and perseverance

- Evidence of a passion and aptitude for research

If you hope to pursue the MD/PhD joint degree, you'll be expected to have clinical experience—through volunteer work, shadowing a physician-scientist, or specific training. Other experiences that admission committee members look for are similar to those of the MD-only candidate: leadership positions, community service activities, and teaching roles.

Finally, it's important to be aware that although significant weight is placed on an applicant's interest and experience in research activities, the applicant is also expected to demonstrate a degree of academic excellence similar to that of people accepted into an MD-only program. For students entering MD/PhD programs in 2014, for example, the mean GPA and total MCAT score were 3.8 and 35.0, respectively (as reported by AMCAS, *www.aamc.org/data/facts/applicantmatriculant*). Keep in mind, though, that the range of GPAs and MCAT scores for accepted applicants is quite broad in conjunction with other selection criteria.

Acceptance Policies

Just as application requirements vary from school to school, so do acceptance policies. Some institutions permit an applicant who is not accepted to the MD/PhD dual-degree program to pursue admission to the MD-only curriculum. Other medical schools will accept applications from MD/PhD candidates only for both degree programs, and failure to gain admittance to one program precludes consideration from another. Because school policies differ, applicants should clarify these matters with individual schools before applying and let admission office staff know of their interest in pursuing an MD-only program (if that is the case) should they not be admitted to the dual-degree program.

Financing MD/PhD Programs

The sources of funding for MD/PhD programs vary from school to school. Many schools offer full support for both the MD and PhD components of their education, including tuition waivers, stipends, and health insurance. At other institutions, different degrees of support are available, sometimes only for the PhD component of the program. Before applying to an MD/PhD dual-degree program, you should know the level of financial assistance available.

A significant amount of funding comes from institutional sources and both individual and institutional grants. The latter include the Medical Scientist Training Program (MSTP) sponsored by the National Institutes of Health (NIH), as well as other NIH grants. The MSTP currently has 45 participating programs with a total of 932 trainees. About 170 positions for new students are available nationwide each year. For more information, go to *www.nigms.nih.gov/Training/InstPredoc/Pages/PredocOverview-MSTP.aspx*. To review the list of medical schools participating in the MSTP, visit *www.nigms.nih.gov/Training/InstPredoc/PredocInst-MSTP.htm*. You may also want to contact the program officials at the institutions of interest and review the schools' websites for complete information.

Bear in mind that although most MD/PhD programs offer support for their students, additional resources are available. Most take the form of competitive applications submitted by the trainee and a research mentor. They include fellowships from both private sources and a number of NIH institutes. You can review the list of these opportunities at *students-residents.aamc.org/applying-medical-school/article/financial-support-md-phd-trainees*.

Gap Year and Career Changers

If you have a significant break between earning your bachelor's degree and applying to medical school, you should use some of that time to gain more research and medically related experience (such as working, shadowing, or volunteering in hospitals and clinics). This will help make you a competitive applicant—you can draw on that experience as you complete your medical school applications and interviews. For more information about gaining research experience, see the Aspiring Docs Fact Sheet called How to Get Lab Experience, *students-residents.aamc.org/applying-medical-school/article/how-get-lab-experience*.

Additional Information

For additional information and guidance about application to and enrollment in combined MD/PhD programs, please visit the AAMC's website on dual-degree programs at *www.aamc.org/mdphd* and contact your pre-health advisor and the MD/PhD program director at the medical schools of interest.

For additional information about clinical specialties, see:

Brass LF, Akabas MH, Burnley LD, Engman DM, Wiley CA, Andersen OS. 2010. Are MD-PhD programs meeting their goals? An analysis of career choices made by graduates of 24 MD-PhD programs. Academic Medicine 2010; 85(4):692–701.

Paik JC, Howard G, Lorenz RG. Postgraduate choices of graduates from medical scientist training programs, 2004–2008. JAMA 2009; 302(12):1271–1273.

Want to Learn More? You can find answers to questions frequently asked by students at *www.aamc.org/ students/research/mdphd/109850/mdphd_faqs.html*.

Worksheets at the end of chapters in this guide are available in fillable PDF format at www.aamc.org/msar-resources.

When researching your options, view the AAMC's table with information on MD/PhD programs online and fill in the chart below to see if you fit the application criteria and may want to apply to the program (*students-residents.aamc.org/choosing-medical-career/careers-medical-research/md-phd-dual-degree-training*).

Program Name	MSPT Funded?	Positions Funded?	Internal MD Students?	Internal PhD Students?	Transfer Students?	Non-U.S. Citizens or Non-State Residents Accepted	GRE Required?	Summer Positions?	Consider Applying?

Chapter 13

U.S. Medical Schools
Accredited by the Liaison Committee on Medical Education (LCME)

Medical School Admission Requirements Website—Complete U.S. Medical School Profiles

For complete, detailed information about each U.S. medical school, including MCAT® and GPA data, school-specific admission requirements and policies, applicant and acceptee statistics, and side-by-side medical school comparisons, purchase a subscription to the Medical School Admission Requirements. For more information about the Medical School Admission Requirements website, a preview of the site, and a complete list of site features, data, and information, visit *www.aamc.org/msar*.

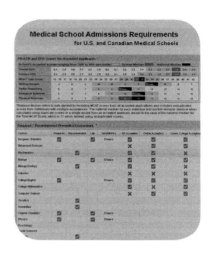

U.S. Medical Schools

Alabama

University of Alabama School of Medicine

University of South Alabama College of Medicine

Arizona

University of Arizona College of Medicine—Phoenix

University of Arizona College of Medicine—Tucson

Arkansas

University of Arkansas for Medical Sciences College of Medicine

California

California Northstate University School of Medicine

Keck School of Medicine of the University of Southern California

Loma Linda University School of Medicine

Stanford University School of Medicine

University of California, Davis, School of Medicine

University of California, Irvine, School of Medicine

University of California, Los Angeles David Geffen School of Medicine

University of California, Riverside, School of Medicine

University of California, San Diego School of Medicine

University of California, San Francisco, School of Medicine

Colorado

University of Colorado School of Medicine

Connecticut

Frank H. Netter MD School of Medicine at Quinnipiac University

University of Connecticut School of Medicine

Yale School of Medicine

District of Columbia

George Washington University School of Medicine and Health Sciences

Georgetown University School of Medicine

Howard University College of Medicine

Florida

Charles E. Schmidt College of Medicine at Florida Atlantic University

Florida International University Herbert Wertheim College of Medicine

Florida State University College of Medicine

University of Central Florida College of Medicine

University of Florida College of Medicine

University of Miami Leonard M. Miller School of Medicine

USF Health Morsani College of Medicine

Georgia

Emory University School of Medicine

Medical College of Georgia at Augusta University

Mercer University School of Medicine

Morehouse School of Medicine

Hawaii

University of Hawaii, John A. Burns School of Medicine

Illinois

Chicago Medical School at Rosalind Franklin University of Medicine & Science

Loyola University Chicago Stritch School of Medicine

Northwestern University The Feinberg School of Medicine

Rush Medical College of Rush University Medical Center

Southern Illinois University School of Medicine

University of Chicago Division of the Biological Sciences, The Pritzker School of Medicine

University of Illinois College of Medicine

Indiana

Indiana University School of Medicine

Iowa

University of Iowa Roy J. and Lucille A. Carver College of Medicine

Kansas

University of Kansas School of Medicine

Kentucky

University of Kentucky College of Medicine

University of Louisville School of Medicine

Louisiana

Louisiana State University School of Medicine in Shreveport

Louisiana State University School of Medicine in New Orleans

Tulane University School of Medicine

Maryland

Johns Hopkins University School of Medicine

Uniformed Services University of the Health Sciences F. Edward Hebert School of Medicine

University of Maryland School of Medicine

Massachusetts

Boston University School of Medicine

Harvard Medical School

Tufts University School of Medicine

University of Massachusetts Medical School

Michigan

Central Michigan University College of Medicine

Michigan State University College of Human Medicine

Oakland University William Beaumont School of Medicine

University of Michigan Medical School

Wayne State University School of Medicine

Western Michigan University Homer Stryker M.D. School of Medicine

Minnesota
Mayo Medical School

University of Minnesota Medical School

Mississippi
University of Mississippi School of Medicine

Missouri
Saint Louis University School of Medicine

University of Missouri—Columbia School of Medicine

University of Missouri—Kansas City School of Medicine

Washington University in St. Louis School of Medicine

Nebraska
Creighton University School of Medicine

University of Nebraska College of Medicine

Nevada
University of Nevada School of Medicine

New Hampshire
Geisel School of Medicine at Dartmouth

New Jersey
Cooper Medical School of Rowan University

Rutgers, New Jersey Medical School

Rutgers, Robert Wood Johnson Medical School

New Mexico
University of New Mexico School of Medicine

New York
Albany Medical College

Albert Einstein College of Medicine

City University of New York School of Medicine

Columbia University College of Physicians and Surgeons

Hofstra Northwell School of Medicine at Hofstra University

Icahn School of Medicine at Mount Sinai

New York Medical College

Jacobs School of Medicine and Biomedical Sciences at the University at Buffalo

New York University School of Medicine

State University of New York Downstate Medical Center College of Medicine

State University of New York Upstate Medical University

Stony Brook University School of Medicine

University of Rochester School of Medicine and Dentistry

Weill Cornell Medicine

North Carolina
The Brody School of Medicine at East Carolina University

Duke University School of Medicine

University of North Carolina at Chapel Hill School of Medicine

Wake Forest University School of Medicine of Wake Forest Baptist Medical Center

North Dakota
University of North Dakota School of Medicine and Health Sciences

Ohio
Case Western Reserve University School of Medicine

Northeastern Ohio Medical University

Ohio State University College of Medicine

University of Cincinnati College of Medicine

The University of Toledo College of Medicine

Wright State University Boonshoft School of Medicine

Oklahoma
University of Oklahoma College of Medicine

Oregon
Oregon Health & Science University School of Medicine

Pennsylvania
The Commonwealth Medical College

Drexel University College of Medicine

Lewis Katz School of Medicine at Temple University

Pennsylvania State University College of Medicine

Raymond and Ruth Perelman School of Medicine at the University of Pennsylvania

Sidney Kimmel Medical College at Thomas Jefferson University

University of Pittsburgh School of Medicine

Puerto Rico
Ponce Health Sciences University School of Medicine

San Juan Bautista School of Medicine

Universidad Central del Caribe School of Medicine

University of Puerto Rico School of Medicine

Rhode Island
The Warren Alpert Medical School of Brown University

South Carolina
Medical University of South Carolina College of Medicine

University of South Carolina School of Medicine

University of South Carolina School of Medicine—Greenville

South Dakota
Sanford School of Medicine, University of South Dakota

Tennessee
East Tennessee State University James H. Quillen College of Medicine

Meharry Medical College

University of Tennessee Health Science Center College of Medicine

Vanderbilt University School of Medicine

Texas
Baylor College of Medicine

McGovern Medical School at the University of Texas Health Science Center at Houston

Texas A&M Health Science Center College of Medicine

Texas Tech University Health Sciences Center Paul L. Foster School of Medicine

Texas Tech University Health Sciences Center School of Medicine

University of Texas at Austin Dell Medical School

University of Texas Medical Branch School of Medicine

The University of Texas School of Medicine at San Antonio

University of Texas Rio Grande Valley School of Medicine

University of Texas Southwestern Medical Center at Dallas Southwestern Medical School

Utah
University of Utah School of Medicine

Vermont
University of Vermont College of Medicine

Virginia
Eastern Virginia Medical School

University of Virginia School of Medicine

Virginia Commonwealth University School of Medicine

Virginia Tech Carilion School of Medicine

Washington
University of Washington School of Medicine

West Virginia
Marshall University Joan C. Edwards School of Medicine

West Virginia University School of Medicine

Wisconsin
Medical College of Wisconsin

University of Wisconsin School of Medicine and Public Health

Chapter 14

Canadian Medical Schools
Accredited by the LCME and by CACMS

Basheer Elsohl
MD Candidate
Queen's University School of Medicine
Class of 2017

Having completed my undergraduate education in Canada, I decided to pursue medical training there as well. Canadian medical school curriculums are similar to those taught in the United States and meet the same LCME requirements. I enjoy focusing on problem-based and simulation-based medical education, as it allows me to practice my skills and hone my knowledge in a risk-free educational setting.

I chose Queen's University because of the exceptional sense of collegiality that is prevalent in the faculty of medicine, as well as its focus on technological innovation in education and hands-on training through early clinical exposure. Despite its large geographical dimensions, Canada only has 17 medical schools. Reflecting Canada's official bilingualism, 13 of these programs are exclusively English-speaking, three are exclusively French-speaking, and one is fully bilingual. Canadian medical schools are united under the Association of Faculties of Medicine of Canada [www.afmc.ca], and all are affiliate members of the Association of American Medical Colleges [www.aamc.org]. All Canadian medical schools are officially accredited by both the U.S. Liaison Committee on Medical Education [www.lcme.org] and the Canadian Committee on Accreditation of Canadian Medical Schools [www.afmc.ca/accreditation].

Selection Criteria

Canadian medical schools vary with respect to the number of years of undergraduate instruction they require of applicants. They also vary in the recommended content covered during premedical undergraduate education. Table 14.1 shows that physics, inorganic and organic chemistry, biology, biochemistry, humanities, and English are the most common required subjects there.

Table 14.1. Subjects Required by Two or More Canadian Medical Schools, 2015–2016 Entering Class*

Required Subject	# of Schools
Biochemistry	4
Biology	6
Calculus	4
College English	2
College Mathematics	3
Humanities	2
Inorganic Chemistry	5
Organic Chemistry	7
Physics	5
Social Sciences	2

*n=17. Figures based on data provided fall 2015. Four of the 17 medical schools (Dalhousie, Northern Ontario, McMaster, and Western Ontario) did not indicate specific course requirements and are not included in the tabulations. Source: AAMC Medical College Admission Requirements website, 2016.

Language of Instruction

Three Canadian medical schools—Laval, Montréal, and Sherbrooke, all located in Quebec province—require students to be fluent in French because all instruction is in that language. Instruction in 13 other schools is in English, and the University of Ottawa offers the MD curriculum in both French and English.

In Canada, universities fall under provincial jurisdiction, and the majority of places in each faculty of medicine are allocated to permanent residents of the province in which the university is located.

Not all faculties of medicine accept applications from international students. Conversely, some faculties of medicine may reserve positions for international students, possibly as part of agreements with foreign governments and institutions. Statistics compiled by the Association of Faculties of Medicine of Canada (*www.afmc.ca*) show that most medical schools admit international students. In 2014–2015, for example, 181 U.S. students applied to 15 schools.

Canadian medical schools that supplied data recorded a 5.5 percent success rate, meaning that 5.5 percent of the U.S. applicants were accepted. In the same year, 302 non-U.S. international students applied to the 15 Canadian medical schools that supplied data, and their success rate was 5.0 percent. The success rate for Canadian applicants to the same schools was 20.0 percent. Additional information about Canadian medical schools can be found in the Association of Faculties of Medicine of Canada publication *Admission Requirements of Canadian Faculties of Medicine* (2015) (*www.afmc.ca/publications/admission-requirements-canadian-faculties-medicine*).

Positions filled by international students in Canadian medical schools are not necessarily subsidized by provincial or territorial governments. This means that international students, including U.S. students, may pay higher tuition and fees than Canadian residents.

Academic Record and Suitability

Although an excellent academic record is a very important factor in gaining admission to a Canadian medical school, admission committees also put a great deal of effort into assessing applicants' suitability for a medical career based on other factors, too. Personal suitability is assessed differently by each school, but in general, personal qualities related to medicine are very important. Applicants who can demonstrate that they possess the qualities considered important in the practice of medicine may sometimes be admitted even if their academic record is not outstanding. Conversely, applicants with outstanding records who don't possess these qualities may not gain a place in medical school.

Most applicants to Canadian medical schools are interviewed before acceptance, so the interview information in Chapter 8 is also relevant for applicants to Canadian medical schools.

Table 14.2. Tuition and Student Fees for 2015–2016 First-Year Students at Canadian Medical Schools (in Canadian Dollars)*

Categories of Students	Range	Average**
In-Province	$4,537–$27,002	$16,096
Canada, Out-of-Province	$7,521–$27,002	$17,910
Visa	$19,441–$68,161	$34,828

*Figures based on data provided in fall 2015.
**Average in-province and out-of-province data were derived from all 17 Canadian schools. Average visa data were derived from eight schools that accept foreign students.
Source: The Association of Faculties of Medicine of Canada, 2015.

Medical College Admission Test® (MCAT®)

Twelve of the 17 Canadian medical schools require applicants to take the MCAT exam: Alberta, British Columbia, Calgary, Dalhousie, Manitoba, McGill, McMaster, Memorial, Queen's, Saskatchewan, Toronto, and Western Ontario.

Tuition and Other Compulsory Fees

Because the medical schools in Canada fall under the jurisdiction of provincial governments, annual tuition and compulsory fees vary considerably. Applicants who reside in the province where the medical school is located may pay annual fees ranging from $4,537 to $27,002, with an average of $16,096 (see Table 14.2). Applicants who are Canadian citizens or permanent residents in a different province may pay fees ranging from $7,521 to $27,002, with an average of $17,910, and foreign student applicants can expect to pay fees ranging from $19,441 to $68,161, with an average of $34,828.

Other Considerations

Canadian faculties of medicine do not discriminate on the basis of race, religion, or gender in admitting new students. The admission of Aboriginal students (First Nations, Inuit, and Métis) is encouraged at Canadian medical schools, and most allocate positions specifically for Aboriginal applicants, including Laval, Sherbrooke, Montréal, McGill, Ottawa, Queen's, McMaster, Western Ontario, Northern Ontario School of Medicine, Saskatchewan, Alberta, and British Columbia.

The number of female applicants has leveled off in recent years, with correspondingly consistent proportions of women in schools' entering classes. Women made up 55 percent of the 2014–2015 applicant pool, and the success rate for women was slightly higher than that for men. The 2014 entering classes at the 15 Canadian medical schools reporting data about male and female matriculants included 55 percent women and 45 percent men. Overall, 20 percent of applicants received at least one offer of admission.

Expenses and Financial Aid

Tuition and student fees for Canadian and non-Canadian students in the 2015 entering class are provided in Table 14.2 and in individual medical school entries on the Medical School Admission Requirements website. Expenses vary from school to school and from student to student. Tuition at several Canadian schools is slightly higher for the first year than for successive years. Some financial aid information is provided in the individual school entries. Eligible Canadian students may apply for a Canadian student loan, or they may apply to the Department of Education in their province for a provincial student loan.

Canadian Medical Schools

Alberta
University of Alberta Faculty of Medicine and Dentistry

University of Calgary Cumming School of Medicine

British Columbia
University of British Columbia Faculty of Medicine

Manitoba
University of Manitoba Faculty of Medicine

Newfoundland
Memorial University of Newfoundland Faculty of Medicine

Nova Scotia
Dalhousie University Faculty of Medicine

Ontario
McMaster University Michael G. DeGroote School of Medicine

Northern Ontario School of Medicine

Queen's University Faculty of Health Sciences

University of Ottawa Faculty of Medicine

University of Toronto Faculty of Medicine

The University of Western Ontario—Schulich School of Medicine & Dentistry

Quebec
Faculty of Medicine Université Laval

McGill University Faculty of Medicine

Université de Montréal Faculty of Medicine

Université de Sherbrooke Faculty of Medicine

Saskatchewan
University of Saskatchewan College of Medicine

 Worksheets at the end of chapters in this guide are available in fillable PDF format at *www.aamc.org/msar-resources*.

Worksheet 14.1
Questions About Canadian Medical Schools to Ask During Interviews

As you research the Canadian medical schools you're interested in attending, use this worksheet to keep track of questions you think you may ask during your interview. Print or save this page for individual schools and review it the night before your interview or bring it with you. You can find many questions here: *www.aamc.org/students/download/175218/data/medical_school_interview.pdf*.

Name of Medical School: _____

Type of Interview: _____

Date of Interview: _____

Questions about

1. Curriculum _____
_____
_____

2. Student Involvement _____
_____
_____

3. Special Programs _____
_____
_____

4. Financial Aid _____
_____
_____

5. Facilities _____
_____
_____

6. Academic Evaluations _____
_____
_____

7. Student Support _____
_____
_____

8. Residency Placements _____
_____
_____

9. Other _____
_____

Acronyms

AAMC
Association of American Medical Colleges
www.aamc.org

AMCAS
American Medical College Application Service®
www.aamc.org/amcas

CiM
Careers in Medicine
www.aamc.org/cim

COA
Cost of Attendance

EDP
Early Decision Program
students-residents.aamc.org/applying-medical-school/article/early-decision-program/

ERAS
Electronic Residency Application Service
www.aamc.org/eras

FAFSA
Free Application for Federal Student Aid
fafsa.ed.gov

FIRST
Financial Information, Resources, Services, and Tools
www.aamc.org/first

GHLO
Global Health Learning Opportunities
www.aamc.org/ghlo

GQ
Graduation Questionnaire

HHMI
Howard Hughes Medical Institute
www.hhmi.org
www.hhmi.org/programs/science-education-research-training

HIPAA
Health Insurance Portability and Accountability Act

LCME
Liaison Committee on Medical Education
www.lcme.org

MCAT
Medical College Admission Test®
www.aamc.org/mcat

Med-MAR
Medical Minority Applicant Registry
www.aamc.org/students/minorities

MSAR
Medical School Admission Requirements
www.aamc.org/msar

MSQ
Matriculating Student Questionnaire

NAAHP
National Association of Advisors for the Health Professions
www.naahp.org

NBME
National Board of Medical Examiners
www.nbme.org

NHSC
National Health Service Corps
nhsc.hrsa.gov

NIH
National Institutes of Health
www.nih.gov
www.training.nih.gov

NRMP
National Resident Matching Program
www.nrmp.org

NSLDS
National Student Loan Data System
www.nslds.ed.gov.

SMDEP
Summer Medical and Dental Education Program
www.smdep.org

TSF
Tuition and Student Fees Survey
services.aamc.org/tsfreports/select.cfm?year_of_study=2016

USMLE
United States Medical Licensing Examination
www.usmle.org

VSAS
Visiting Student Application Service
www.aamc.org/vsas